PRAISE FOR *THE POTENTIATOR*

"You might call this book the new 'Vocabulary of Victory.' Want to play at your best? Read at your best. And start with this book."

Ron Tite, author of *Think. Do. Say.: How to Seize Attention and Build Trust in a Busy, Busy World*

"Leadership legacies are not just about winning the game. Leaders create legacies when they transform the game. We're all in the business of creating breakthroughs with others. In this book, Mike Lipkin shows you a practical approach to turning fantasies into dreams, and dreams into legacies. I love it!"

Silvio Stroescu, president, BMO InvestorLine, at BMO Financial Group

"Mike Lipkin has been one of my Potentiators for many years. The practices outlined in *The Potentiator* will help me improve on the things that really matter. I had fun reading this book and encourage you to do the same!"

Mike Parra, CEO, Americas, at DHL Express

"Whether it's on the page or on a stage, Mike Lipkin is always timely, relevant, provocative, insightful and inspiring. *The Potentiator* is a tactical and strategic roadmap to creating breakthroughs for yourself and for the people around you."

Martin Perelmuter, co-founder and president, Speakers' Spotlight

D0111423

"I've known Mike Lipkin for years and he is a smart, talented guy. If you're comfortable, you're not growing. This book is the roadmap to being bold, brave and successful!"

Bruce MacLellan, president and CEO, Proof Strategies

"I've had the pleasure of collaborating many times with Mike Lipkin, whether he is presenting his insights at a workshop, acting as a mentor or sharing his personal journey to encourage and educate. I love reading his books because they're a treat for my brain and my heart. His latest offering, *The Potentiator*, is signature Mike: he motivates, encourages and inspires readers as they journey toward positive change. Change is hard work but imminently possible. *The Potentiator* illuminates the path."

Dr. Diane McIntosh, chief neuroscience officer, Telus, and author of *This Is Depression*

"Mike Lipkin has always provided me with awesome guidance. I'm inspired about creating my next breakthrough moment. After reading this book, you will be too."

Karen Werger, CPA, CA, CBV, global leader valuations and modeling, Deloitte LLP

"*The Potentiator* is essential reading for anyone who wants to build trust with others. The Potentiator Practices that Mike Lipkin shares in this book are priceless."

Lisa Kimmel, chair and CEO, Edelman Canada

"The breakthrough mindset defined in this book will help you magnetize success. I have already begun to apply the Five Potentiator Practices to great effect. I'm inspired!"

Christian Roy, executive vice president, health division, at Tank Worldwide, a WPP Company

"*The Potentiator* offers an inspirational and uplifting approach that helps the reader make game-changing realizations page after page. Mike Lipkin has created a unique modality to guide others toward their own self-mastery so that they can pay it forward."

Karen Azlen, founder and CEO, Introduction Capital Inc.

"I tend to like books that push me out of my comfort zone. Books and stories that make me reflect on who I am, where I have come from and where I am going. Most important are the *why* and the *how*. Mike Lipkin, through *The Potentiator*, has created a blueprint for embracing the journey to be your absolute best, regardless of your age, profession or how you define successful living. I plan to re-read this book over and over to challenge me and help me make the most of my life."

Lee Cooper, CEO, Shields Health Solutions

"Early in my career, Mike Lipkin helped me unlock my leadership potential. *The Potentiator* expresses Mike's best insights in ways that are immediately actionable."

Dani Reiss, president and CEO, Canada Goose Inc.

"Mike Lipkin, you have done it again! Another great set of learnings, habits, coaching and darn right irritations. My personal and professional success is a testament to your years of work on me. I love all five of the Potentiator Practices. This book is a must-read for all of us aspiring Potentiators."

Kim Yost, president and CEO, Mega Group Inc.

"I have known Mike Lipkin for two decades. He has inspired countless readers and listeners to self-actualize in their chosen profession, providing practical roadmaps and stories that inspire. *The Potentiator* is Mike's most data-driven motivational text. It's filled with useful insights and I know you will enjoy reading it."

Michael Adams, author and president of the Environics group of companies

THE POTENTIATOR

THE

MIKE LIPKIN

POTENTIATOR

How to Create Breakthroughs With Others In a Post-Pandemic World

ENVIRONICS/LIPKIN

Cataloguing in publication information is available from Library and Archives Canada.

ISBN 978-1-7751225-3-1 (book)
ISBN 978-1-7751225-4-8 (ebook)
ISBN 978-1-7751225-5-5 (audiobook)

Page Two
pagetwo.com

Writing/research services provided by Matthew O'Grady
Copyedited by James Harbeck
Cover design by Peter Cocking
Interior design by Peter Cocking and Setareh Ashrafologhalai
Interior illustrations by Ian Herring

mikelipkin.com

A life is not important except in the impact it has on other lives.

JACKIE ROBINSON

Contents

Introduction

HIS NAME is Tim. He owns an advertising agency in Switzerland. He is 51 years old. He is of medium height. He has a slight build—one that's growing soft with age—and he favours nondescript glasses. His hairline has been receding for over a decade, and his curly brown hair now sits high on the top of his head. Tim is not handsome, but not ugly. He is ordinary.

Until he speaks. Then, his entire person lights up. Tim's insights shine through. His humour *sparkles*. His charisma *crackles*. His physical appearance transforms into that of a rock star. He *magnetizes* others to him. Tim's words are well chosen, his ideas are well formed—and his track record is well established.

I've been working with Tim for over a decade. We have partnered on multiple marquee assignments around the world—and the assignments have gone well for one simple reason: Tim helps me to play at my best. When Tim is around,

I find another gear; I reach another level; I discover another dimension.

The impact is reciprocal: I also coach Tim on how to lead his people and captivate his clients. I help him see his blind spots so that he can discover opportunities hidden from view. It's a mutuality of interests that magnifies *both* of our successes.

Here's my question to you: Who is *your* Tim? Who makes you more powerful? Who elevates your game? Who helps you play at your best? Who is plugging you into your full potential? Who is the superhero whose superpower is to turn you into a superhero as well?

Who is your Potentiator?

You can have more than one Potentiator. You can be the Potentiator for more than one person. But we're only as good as the Potentiators we purposefully place in our lives.

Sometimes they cross our paths serendipitously. We experience their magic for a brief moment before they move on—like catching lightning in a bottle. Ultimate success comes from forming an enduring relationship with them. It isn't easy.

Potentiators are drawn to potential that is determined to realize itself. You have to demonstrate it before they help you develop it. And it takes one to know one. Potentiators pursue other Potentiators. They play together and empower each other. They are always the students and always the teachers. They are intentional and purposeful in their relationships. No jerks, shirkers, sloths, takers, fakers, wimps, quitters, cynics, bullies, bigots, hermits or cruisers allowed.

Potentiators are an exclusive club that anyone can join. The price of entry isn't education, income or connections;

it's the desire to create breakthroughs by helping others play at their best. It's as simple and as complicated as that. If you want it badly enough, you'll find ways to make it happen. This book is one of them.

I define a *breakthrough* as an action that moves someone through an obstacle. Or it's a sudden insight that enables someone to achieve a remarkable result. Or it's a personal victory over doubt that liberates someone from their fear. Or it's a decisive discovery that precipitates extraordinary progress. Or it's the accomplishment of significant personal success. In short, a breakthrough is situational. It's whatever others need to play at their best in that moment.

Until now, you may not even have been conscious of your desire to create breakthroughs by helping others play at their best. It may even sound grandiose or hyperbolic to you. After all, in a world where excellence is a given, it's hard enough just being good enough. Now that it's on your radar, it sounds obvious, doesn't it? But everything is obvious once it's been thought of. And haven't you always wanted to be a superhero? So have other people. You can be the superhero who makes them superheroes: the Potentiator.

I will show you that becoming the Potentiator doesn't require more work. It requires the *right* work. It means focusing on the things that count—so you can say no to the things that don't. As the Potentiator, you won't be derailed by distraction. You'll be driven by the thrill of discovery. You'll be inspired to achieve unprecedented results with others.

The Potentiator doesn't succeed at others' expense; the Potentiator succeeds at others' *success.*

A New Vocabulary of Power, Opportunity and Possibility

Every year, thousands of words are added to the Oxford Dictionary—and thousands more are revised, bringing new meaning or new pronunciations to time-honoured words. The world's leading lexicographer updates its database quarterly. Here are just four of the almost 9,000 words added or updated in 2021:

digital assistant, n.: "A (usually hand-held) portable computer; esp. one that combines the functions of an electronic organizer with the capacity for networking."

Generation Z, n.: "The generation of people born between the late 1990s and early 2010s, regarded as having attitudes or values which differ from those of the preceding generation (Generation Y), particularly with respect to having grown up in the era of widespread use of digital technology (esp. the internet and social media)."

social distance, v.: "transitive (reflexive) and intransitive. To keep a certain physical distance from, or limit physical contact with, another person or people in order to avoid catching or transmitting an infectious disease, or as one of a number of public health measures designed to inhibit its spread."

allyship, n.: "The state or condition of being or having an ally (in various senses). Now chiefly: *spec.* the state or condition of being a person who supports the rights of a minority or marginalized group without being a member of it."

These are words that were created to define new concepts—and during Covid-19, there were lots of new concepts to describe our dramatically rewired lives. The existing vocabulary we had access to was insufficient, so someone made up a new word, or a new meaning, that has been accepted as a legitimate expression of the English language.

Each one of us—you, me, everyone you meet every day—is involved in this process of word creation all the time. Our existing vocabulary needs to constantly expand in order to accommodate our new challenges and realities. If the word doesn't currently exist, we can even make it up, knowing that if we explain it clearly enough, it could become part of the lexicon.

That's what I'm doing with *Potentiator*, a word that hasn't been used outside the world of medical science. In that context, a potentiator is something that potentiates: an agent that increases the strength or impact of another drug or biological effect. I'm redeploying the word into the arena of human effectiveness and high performance.

In this world, the Potentiator is not a thing or substance. It is a person who increases other people's strength and effectiveness; someone who brings people together so they can achieve more than they could separately; someone who helps actualize others' dreams; someone who produces more energy than they consume; someone who creates breakthroughs by helping others play at their best.

The Potentiator, in other words, is an everyday superhero. But unlike Superman or Spider-Man, who can only be the super-personas of Clark Kent or Peter Parker, the Potentiator is someone *any one of us* can be—if we develop our own personal superpowers. We all have these powers, but not all of us use them. It's time to take action.

I love the sound of "Potentiator." It's the sound of getting things done and making the future real. Just by saying it, you feel potent. It is pronounced "puh-ten-shee-eight-or." Say it aloud. Notice what you need to do with your face and your mouth. You need to purse your lips, then smile—and smile again if you're saying it really expressively! You cannot say "Potentiator" and not become animated. It's the kind of word that becomes self-fulfilling the moment that you utter it.

The Highest Accolade

There is no higher accolade than being recognized as someone who helps others play at their best. It's the essence of a great coach, leader, mentor, partner, team member, colleague or friend. It's also the secret to everybody else's success. No one achieves anything significant without the contribution of an extraordinary person in their corner.

All of us have helped others play at their best at some point. We've all said or done the right thing at the right time. We were there for others when they needed us most. We lifted them up when they were down. We inspired them to carry on when they wanted to give up. We shined a light for them in a moment of darkness.

My question for you is: *How often?* How often are you helping others play at their best? Is it a habit? Is it an activity that you're known for? Do people naturally turn to you because

In *every* meeting, we train people how to expect us to be in the next meeting.

they know you'll be there for them when they need you most? Do you proactively look for opportunities to potentiate others? Or is it a sometime, maybe, when-I-can, fluke, occasional, coincidental kind of endeavour?

Golf is addictive because, in every round, every player is capable of one shot that is worthy of Tiger Woods. Very few can consistently reproduce that calibre of performance. Only world-class professionals have the talent, training and discipline to play at that level. Being the Potentiator is like that too. Everyone can do it now and then, but only a select few can do it all the time. That's what you're here for now: to become so proficient at potentiating others that others call you their MVP—most valuable person. They consult with you before marquee moments or key quests. They regard you as indispensable to their life or business. For them, you are the Potentiator.

In *every* meeting, we train people how to expect us to be in the next meeting. Every word and action shapes others' perception of us. In their minds, we are the sum total of all the direct and indirect experience they have had with us. Being the Potentiator means purposefully engaging with people in such a way that they regard you as someone who will help them play at their best.

The Key Is to Be Bold

Every act is a cause set in motion. If a butterfly flaps its wings in Borneo, it can create a hurricane in Hawaii. The right action at the right moment can cause colossal consequences.

It could be Rosa Parks refusing to move to the back of the bus in 1955. Or it could be Jackie Robinson breaking major league baseball's colour line, when he started at first base for the Brooklyn Dodgers in 1947. Or maybe it's Nobel Prize winner Malala Yousafzai deciding to keep going to school even after she was shot by the Taliban in 2012.

These are individuals who changed the world. But they're also just people who took a *bold step* when it was required of them. They were not tentative or hesitant. They understood that they needed to create their breakthrough. Their resolve enabled miracles to occur. As the poet Johann Wolfgang von Goethe allegedly wrote (as translated by John Anster), "What you can do, or dream you can, begin it, / Boldness has genius, power, and magic in it."

I love the Cambridge English Dictionary's definition of *boldness*: "A brave and confident way of behaving that shows no fear." It doesn't mean that there *is* no fear; it means that your behaviour *shows* no fear. As Jim Loehr and Tony Schwartz wrote in "The Making of a Corporate Athlete" in the January 2001 issue of the *Harvard Business Review*, "Effective acting produces precisely the same physiology that real emotions do. All great athletes understand this instinctively. If they carry themselves confidently, they will eventually start to feel confident, even in highly stressful situations. That's why we train our corporate clients to 'act as if'—consciously creating the look on the outside that they want to feel on the inside."

Simply making the decision to be bold can create breakthroughs. Boldness is kinetic. It demands action. It cannot coexist with coasting or procrastinating. It's the antithesis of ambivalence. It also liberates you from the temptation to do nothing. There is no such thing as a bold spectator or a bold "wait-and-watcher."

Everyone is bold at some point in their lives. The first time you ask someone out on a date, present yourself at a job interview, decide to have a child, ask for a raise or a promotion, travel to an exotic destination, volunteer for a great cause, help someone in a crisis, stand up for what you believe, immigrate to a new country or move to a new city, you are bold. The challenge is to increase your frequency of bold moves until being bold becomes a habit.

That said, I'm not going to pretend that creating bold breakthroughs is easy. Despite your diligence and determination, every breakthrough will be earned by doing the hard things that others are afraid to do. To act boldly is usually the *opposite* of what we are trying to accomplish—which is to be prudent in every situation, to minimize risk, to be wise. It takes nerve to overcome the unspoken norms that inhibit our willingness to dare to venture into the unknown.

However, being prudent and being bold are actually perfectly aligned. *Prudent* means acting in a way that considers the consequences of one's actions, showing care for the future. It doesn't mean being timid or reticent in the face of daunting challenges and opportunities. The Potentiator takes on the responsibility of creating breakthroughs with others. They are willing to live with a higher level of risk than their less impactful counterparts. In fact, their personal mission depends on it. It's only prudent to know that there will always be unknowns that cannot be anticipated.

We've all known people who "seek forgiveness, not permission." But the rulebreakers are not the rule. For example, in the 2019 Environics Research Canadian Social Values Survey, two-thirds of Canadians said they would seek permission first, not forgiveness later—even when they had to get something done quickly. Only 20 percent of the population was willing to incur the wrath of others in pursuit of their desired outcomes—and their behaviours were driven more often by selfish motives.

The Potentiator, on the other hand, is appropriately inappropriate. They seize the moment to shatter shibboleths when they believe intrepid action is called for—just like you're about to do now. It's time.

The Power of Gumption and Chutzpah

As the Potentiator, you understand that not every bold step leads to a breakthrough. But every breakthrough begins with a bold step. That's why you default to being bold. You nurture your gumption and chutzpah. Just saying these two words is almost enough to invest you with their power: "Gumption and chutzpah!"

Gumption is the ability to decide the best thing to do and then to do it with energy and determination. Chutzpah is a charming word that means shameless audacity; it means not being afraid or embarrassed to say or do things that may shock, surprise, dismay or annoy others.

What would you do if you had the gumption and chutzpah to do it? What risks do you know you must take but haven't yet taken? What is the price of your inaction? How many breakthroughs are waiting in the wings because you haven't activated them yet? How many people are depending on you to help them create their breakthroughs? What will it take for you to potentiate their success? How much capacity do you have that is going unused? How much capacity do you want to take to your grave? Or do you want to be fully used up when your time is over?

At a micro-personal level, creating bold breakthroughs means proactively creating your own "peak experiences" every day. A peak experience is one that animates your spirit: it reminds you about the meaning of miracles, encourages you to create more and causes others to stop, look and wonder. Sometimes, the bold breakthrough is a giant leap forward; sometimes, it's going further than you have ever been before or making a significant pivot. Often, it's simply sustaining your mojo in the face of adversity.

Christopher Reeve, the actor who played Superman, fractured his neck at the first and second cervical vertebrae in a horseback-riding accident in 1995. Completely paralyzed from the neck down, Reeve threw himself into every available therapy: sessions on a tilt table that allowed him to stand upright and bear weight, workouts to strengthen his neck and shoulders and treadmill training in which he was suspended over a rolling belt to get his legs moving in a rough gait. But while the regimen kept up his muscle mass—and his spirits—it had no real effect on function, until one day in September 2000 when he discovered he could move his left index finger.

By 2002, he could move the other fingers of his left hand, too, as well as his right wrist. He could straighten his arms and legs, and in a swimming pool initiate a step and push off from the wall. And he could survive for up to two hours off his respirator. News of his progress gripped the paralysis community. Scientists believed that even if new cells aren't growing, therapy may help the spine make the most of the ones it has. Reeve is quoted as saying, "I may be an isolated case, but that shows we no longer know the limits of recovery. If we don't know, why not assume there are none?" For Reeve, moving his fingers created a bold breakthrough; together with his physicians, he worked incessantly to achieve that miracle.

In the past couple of years, we've become acutely aware of the miracles of modern medicine. Take the example of Katalan "Kati" Kariko, a 66-year-old Hungarian-born scientist at the University of Pennsylvania who is considered one of the heroes in the development of a Covid-19 vaccine. After years of toil in various labs across the United States—evangelizing when others wouldn't listen about the possibilities for messenger RNA, or mRNA, as a means of making vaccines— Kariko and her collaborator, Dr. Drew Weissman, were able to lay the foundation for the highly effective and widely used mRNA vaccines developed by Pfizer-BioNTech and Moderna.

"She was, in a positive sense, kind of obsessed with the concept of messenger RNA," said Dr. Anthony Fauci, director of the National Institute of Allergy and Infectious Diseases, in an April 2021 profile of Kariko in the *New York Times.* Fauci thinks her mRNA research is going to be nothing less than transformative for the scientific world. "It is already transforming for Covid-19, but also for other vaccines. H.I.V.— people in the field are already excited. Influenza, malaria."

Vaccines used to take years or decades to develop; in the case of both the Pfizer and Moderna vaccines, each came to market in under a year. The bold breakthrough that has saved

Struggle
is the essential
ingredient
of achievement.

———————

millions of lives around the world would not have happened without the gumption—and the chutzpah—of an otherwise unassuming university scientist, as well as all the other healthcare heroes who brought the miracle to life.

Learn to License Yourself—and Celebrate the Struggle

A licence is a permit from a recognized authority to own or use something—to practice a particular trade or engage in a particular activity. Your driver's licence is in your wallet. Your professional licence may be hanging on your wall. Your licence to create bold breakthroughs, however, is in your mind. You have the power vested in you by your own authority.

No one else can give you this licence—and no one can take it away. Either you use it or you will lose it. As the Potentiator, you take your responsibilities seriously. You're acutely aware of the privilege and pleasure that come with the position. That's why you never neglect your role. Think of the people who have been the Potentiator for you. They are never casual about their interactions with you. Their agenda is always to create breakthroughs with you. Even in the most relaxed situations, the focus is: "How can we do this better together?"

Of course, no bold breakthrough comes easily—just ask Kati Kariko about the many obstacles she's faced over a decades-long scientific career. But struggle is the essential ingredient of achievement. It signals that you're pushing your boundaries. Until you struggle with anything, you don't know how much potential you're leaving unexplored. Anything that comes too easily doesn't stretch your capacity. The secret is to celebrate the struggle, not condemn it. It's the pain that precedes the breakthrough. The bigger the goals, the greater the agony.

At some point, however, the struggle may be stronger than you are. You may feel like you've lost your magic or potency. You stop expecting to win because you're experiencing too many losses. This can be especially disturbing when you're not used to losing at all. I often coach executives with an unblemished record of career wins. Their career may have spanned 30 years without a notable failure—but when failure comes, as it always does, it hits them hard.

For those who get stuck in a slump, they soon start to *anticipate* a loss—with every undesirable outcome building negative momentum. The repeated pattern of undesirable outcomes thrusts them into a "loser's mindset." They feel like they're in reverse—and desperately want to switch gears—but losing has, for them, become a self-fulfilling prophecy.

That's when you need your personal slump buster. It's a mantra you can utter, a declaration you can make, a book you can read, a person you can talk to, a video you can watch, an action you can take or a target you can aim at. It enables you to forget the last defeat and focus on the empowering move that will propel you in the right direction.

Ken Ravizza, co-author of the book *Heads-Up Baseball: Playing the Game One Pitch at a Time*, makes the point succinctly: "Forget the last game, forget the last play and forget the excuses." The only pitch that matters is the next one. A core theme that runs through the entire book is the capacity to let go of what drags you down so you can take hold of what lifts you up. Don't stumble on obstacles that are behind you.

FLAP: Finish Like a Professional

In any professional sport, it's in the late stages of a game when the most points are scored. That's when the stronger side's superiority asserts itself. They get better as the game goes longer. They find a higher gear as their competitors fade. They sustain their zest for winning despite their fatigue.

It's the same in the games of life and business. Potentiators step up as others are stepping down. They know they will be defined by how they finish. To quote Alec Baldwin's character in the classic 1992 movie *Glengarry Glen Ross*, "Coffee's for closers only." The last nine yards is the territory of champions. Winning is not for wimps. It's the refusal to stop until the final whistle blows that earns victory.

I know that by the time the final whistle blows—when you've read this book, from cover to cover—you too will be the Potentiator. You will have a deep understanding, if not mastery, of the five Potentiator Practices explored in the coming chapters. But fair warning: this is not going to be an entirely peaceful or pain-free experience. There is no comfortable way to become the Potentiator. You will be rocked back. You will struggle. You will bump up against your self-imposed limits before you break through them. Complacency is not the birthplace of breakthroughs. But neither is angst. The pain that you may experience is the kind that signifies your growth. Sometimes, as John Mellencamp says, it "hurts so good" because it's truly good for you.

The Five Potentiator Practices

I conduct extensive leadership coaching with C-level executives across North America. I'm often amazed by how much they know about their businesses—and how little they know about themselves. They have an instinctive understanding of what drives them and informs their thinking, but they struggle to explicitly articulate their inner worlds. They just haven't taken the time to shine a light on those areas. Many of them don't even think it's important. They regard it as an indulgence. As one leader told me, "I'm not into navel-gazing. I'd rather focus on the opportunities in front of me."

Although this leader has been extremely successful, he approached me because he feels like he has hit the limit of his capacity. Together, we're discovering the next breakthrough from within—just like I'm going to do with you.

There is a reason that I originated the term Potentiator *Practices*. They are actions that you must take repeatedly—and frequently—to master them. Practicing means systematically exercising for the purpose of acquiring skill or proficiency. It's not a dress rehearsal or dry run for the real thing; it *is* the real thing. It is playing the games of life and using each game to become even better the next time that game is played.

Billie Jean King, the tennis champion, said, "Champions win when things are not quite right." Imperfect external circumstances call forth extraordinary internal qualities to produce remarkable results. In other words, our inner game determines our outer game. Of course, it's easier to win when the stars align. But the great ones unleash their brilliance in the face of crisis, confusion or chaos.

Now is not the time to withdraw or pull back. It's a time of unprecedented opportunity—if you're willing to stretch for it. When you stretch, you expand your mind or your body to its full length. You play big and you stand tall. You increase your mental and physical flexibility and mobility. You reduce your tightness and pain. A mind that is stretched is one that keeps on growing.

Just as a recipe has both ingredients and sequence, there is a specific flow to the Potentiator Practices.

The first Potentiator Practice is **Know Your Game.** It is foundational to everything else. It's about being an authority in your field—so you become the go-to person for those in the know.

The second Potentiator Practice is **Build Robust Resilience.** It is building the capacity to turn every setback into a launchpad. It's about thriving in the crunch moments so you can empower others to capitalize on their crises.

The third Potentiator Practice is **Grow Courageous Creativity.** It is cultivating the ability to see the world in new ways and the commitment to shape it the way you see it. It's about liberating yourself to live your vision so you can free others to pursue their passion.

The fourth Potentiator Practice is **Communicate Like a Champion.** It is developing the talent to transfer just the right information and inspiration to others. It's about using all your gifts to excite others into successful action.

The fifth Potentiator Practice is **Cultivate Close Connections.** It is mastering the art of accelerating trust and intimacy. It's about becoming so integral to the wellbeing of others that they *choose* to invest their time with you.

In every chapter, I assign you specific steps to master each Potentiator Practice. I call them "Make Your Breakthrough" because any one of them could elevate you to the next level. Stop and ponder each one. Then do something, even if it seems awkward or out of character with who you believe yourself to be. You'll discover things about yourself that could redefine those beliefs. Every action is a deposit on the person you want to become.

There are mind-blowing insights and stories ahead. You have to read them to believe them. Don't worry if you're ready. Don't even worry about getting ready. Just get started. Let's go.

1

The First
Potentiator Practice
Know Your
Game

Game: a physical or mental competition conducted according to rules; an area of expertise; willing or ready to proceed; having or showing a resolute spirit.

ADAPTED FROM MERRIAM-WEBSTER.COM

W E ALWAYS know it when we see it. It's a sight that inspires us while reassuring us. It reminds us of what's possible while motivating us to pursue our version of it. It's a source of wonder that we wish we had.

I'm talking about someone who knows their game so well they define the way it should be played. It's Roger Federer, Serena Williams, Tom Brady, Bill Belichick or Misty Copeland. It's Bill Gates, Tim Cook, Margaret Atwood, Stephen King, Anna Wintour, Oprah Winfrey or Martin Scorsese. Pick your icon.

It could also be the high school teacher who made you love to learn, the coach who prepared you to compete, the mentor who helped you navigate your path or the boss who empowered you to win. It's the elite cast of everyday people who are palpably great at what they do, no matter what they do.

These are folks who have mastered their inner game. They have the clarity of their convictions and the power of their skillsets. They know what they want. They know how to get it. And they know what they need to give others. They are integrated. All of their parts are firing in formation.

When you talk to people like this, you sense their congruence. There is no doubt emanating from them. They don't waste time or lose momentum second-guessing themselves.

They might be wrong, but they're never hesitant. They would follow themselves. Would you follow you?

Life is a game and we're all players on its field. In reality, though, there's actually *more* than one field to contend with. Whether in life or in business, there are three domains you have to carefully navigate, each and every day:

What we know that we know.

What we know that we *don't* know.

What we *don't* know that we don't know.

The first domain is the foundation of our strength. It's our safe place. It enables us to stride confidently forward—the collection of a lifetime of experience. The second domain is where we either choose to increase our expertise or hire others to perform the role. The third domain is decisive: it represents the biggest area of our future lives; it's ever-changing; it's undefinable. But it also represents infinite possibility.

If you can embrace not knowing what you don't know—and being excited about discovering it every day—you will reap the rewards of being the Potentiator.

The paradox of *knowing your game* means being open to not knowing what you don't know. Why? Because that's what magnetizes knowledge to us. The most exhilarating exclamation you can make is "Huh, I never knew that!" or "Wow, I never thought about it that way before!" or "I could never have imagined!"

Put another way: what you know you know—and what you know you don't know—are like handfuls of sand on a beach full of unknown unknowns.

Covid-19 magnified this truth. Many of the most seemingly omniscient scientists were blindsided by the pandemic. For each of us, our life was upended by it. Ultimately, though, we were transformed. Just like you, I'm living a life that was unimaginable at the beginning of 2020. And yet, here I am: the Potentiator. I am coaching thousands of people how to thrive in a post-pandemic reality.

I marvel at being a rookie and a guru at the same time. In fact, it's the unknown unknowns that make this miracle possible. Growth-minded people everywhere are acutely aware of the tsunami of surprises bearing down on them. They are expecting the unexpected. They are cognizant of their ignorance but they're not constrained by it. On the contrary, their fascination outweighs their fear. After all, they've made it this far—and they're curious to go further.

Knowing your game, therefore, is a function of attitude and action. The base level is knowing what you need to know—and that starts with *you*. But that's only 20 percent of the equation; the other 80 percent is knowing how to explore the unknown unknowns, with the understanding that they change every day—in everything you do.

Know Who You Are and What You're Capable Of: Be Self-Savvy

Everything about you is either attracting or repelling other people. Just as oil doesn't mix with water, you won't mix well with everyone. There are ingrained traits that will alienate people no matter what you do. It could be the way you look, the way you sound or even the way you smell. That's just the way it is. Optics, acoustics and pheromones are organic signals that bypass our rational faculties.

About 20 percent of the population will be biased against you from the start. You will remind them of what's wrong with their world. You will represent what they believe is reprehensible. No matter what you do, you will deepen their antipathy toward you. These are your detractors. Don't waste your time or energy trying to convert them to you.

About 20 percent of people will like you at first sight. You are a symbol of their hopes, dreams or happiness. They want what they believe you to be. They're your mobilizers. They're your champions waiting to happen. All they need is guidance from you to help them contribute to your success. Maximize your investment in them.

The middle 60 percent of people are indifferent to your charms and flaws. They are unmoved by you one way or the other. They are your neutrals. They can become assets or liabilities, depending on their interaction with you. Use your discretion as to how much effort you should invest in turning them on to you.

The ability to understand the intersection of your principles, your effect on others and the role you must play is what I call "being self-savvy." Simply put, self-savvy means being perceptive, well-informed and shrewd, having practical knowledge and exercising good judgement. It means that you know what to do and how to do it. You're attuned to your own values and priorities while you gauge the nature and wellbeing of the people around you. It's your internal and external radar—constantly sweeping your immediate environment and instructing you on immediate action.

This is particularly important given the new world we live in—often referred to as a TUNA world: full of Turbulence, Uncertainty, Novelty and Ambiguity. In the post-Covid reality,

Breakthroughs rarely happen in our comfort zones or on our own schedules.

the Potentiator needs to master situations that are unprecedented and unfamiliar. Breakthroughs rarely happen in our comfort zones or on our own schedules. We need to take the time to review, reflect and reset, but we also need to move fast. In a TUNA world, there are no do-overs. A split second may be all the time we have. Opportunities happen in real time, and we need to respond accordingly. Speed trumps perfection.

The Power of Personal Principles

There are truths that are universally accepted or self-evident: the sun rises in the east; everybody dies; water is essential to life; spring always follows winter; for every action, there is an equal and opposite reaction; water boils at 212°F (100°C) and if you put your hand in it, you'll burn yourself. You cannot argue with these *external* truths. They are undeniable.

Internal truths, on the other hand, are unquestionably accepted or uniquely evident *only* to us. They are our personal principles and they are more influential than any external truth. Our actions often disregard external truths. We sometimes think we can defy the laws of gravity or ageing. But we *always* follow our personal principles—even when we think we don't. Any time you find yourself acting in opposition to a personal principle, reflect on your actions. If you're honest with yourself, you will note that it's not really a personal principle; it may be one that you think you *should* have or *would like* to have, but it's not one that you currently *do* have.

The vast majority of people with whom I work cannot explicitly define their personal principles. They are conditioned to follow certain cultural guidelines. They are moulded by society's view of right or wrong. They understand their legal obligations and the penalties for not fulfilling them. They have inherited internal truths that they in turn pass down to their children. They have a general sense of how to act in a way that is appropriate in their environment. That instinct ensures their survival. It could even guide their success. But it won't enable them to systematically be at their best.

To be the Potentiator, you need to have an acute grasp of your personal principles. You need to be the author of your own story. You need to be conscious of your past but the creator of your future. You need to understand that demography isn't destiny: at any moment, you can "choose to choose." You cannot always control your circumstances, but you can always control your response to your circumstances.

MAKE YOUR BREAKTHROUGH

A Test of Principles

What are your personal principles? Write down your top 10 personal principles, in order of priority. Review your behaviours and ask yourself: What personal principles motivated you to act like that? Begin by writing down all the principles that you believe you live by. Then prioritize and prune them. Some of your principles may even be in conflict with each other. Be truthful with yourself. Perhaps you need to make a list of aspirational principles that you want to follow but don't yet. Don't worry if the list isn't immediately clear for you. This isn't a race. Live with it for a little bit.

My personal principles are:

1 Continuous growth—every day is Discovery Day

2 Joy and fulfillment—pursue happiness and be fully
   self-actualized

3 Health and vitality—it's about physical wellbeing
   and feeling hyper-alive

4 Contribution to others—give back and share the bounty

5 Wealth generation—money is a means to a lot of ends

6 Personal recognition—others' admiration is valida-
   tion of myself

7 Freedom—being able to choose how to live, work
   and play

8 Variety—change is good and different is better

9 Acceptance—everyone is right as long as they
   don't do wrong to others

10 Courage—overcome fear to achieve my dreams

In a TUNA world, you need your personal principles,
that sense of self, to guide you. Sometimes you will
find yourself in a strange place—and sometimes in
a strange place, you'll find yourself. But know that
everyone is navigating their way through a place that
is strange to them. We're all pioneers in the new realities. We're all improvising our strategies to survive
and thrive. It can feel like we're alone in this brave
new world, but we're all in it together. Pre-Covid, we
may have been able to cruise along on autopilot.
Post-Covid, we're recalibrating our internal operating
systems to master the next normal. Those who don't
will go the way of the dodo.

If You're Going to Sit, Sit. If You're Going to Stand, Stand. But Don't Wobble

Ambivalence literally means having mixed feelings or contradictory ideas about someone or something. It's the absence of personal principles that default you one way or the other. It's a powerlessness that leads to paralysis. It's the antithesis of being the Potentiator.

We cannot always do the right thing, but we can always do what's right. If you're consciously following your personal principles by reflecting on your actions, you'll never ask yourself the worst questions in the world: "Why did I do that? What was I thinking? What got into me?"

Without your personal principles to guide you, or if they conflict with each other, you'll feel weak and confused. Your lack of confidence will show. You'll look and sound tentative. Others will recognize your hesitation and mirror it. They will be infected by your uncertainty, and they'll avoid you wherever they can. On the other hand, passion is persuasive. Strength is seductive. Conviction is compelling.

Discern Your Impact

As a motivator and coach, I am constantly pitching my potential contribution to prospects' success. It usually begins with an email requesting me to submit my proposal, or it's an email that I initiated. It could also be an inbound or outbound phone call that precipitates the interaction.

Sometimes, it goes exactly the way I want it to. I respond with a proposal that is favourably received, or I establish

Passion is persuasive. Strength is seductive. Conviction is compelling.

immediate traction over the phone. I follow up with a face-to-face meeting, where I establish rapport and communicate my masterful understanding of how to solve the clients' problem. In short order, I close the deal and begin a fabulous, lucrative relationship. These clients are my mobilizers. They love what I represent. They are yesses waiting to happen. It's a beautiful thing.

Sometimes, it goes nowhere. I hit a dead end. I may not even hear anything from the prospect again. It's over before it began. Even if I make it to a meeting, I'm a dead man walking. These clients are my detractors. It's horrible and it never gets easier to swallow.

Other times, it becomes a sheer test of stamina. Eight steps forward, seven steps back. Just when I think I've clinched the deal, it slips away again. I step into the arena over and over again. Twenty percent of the time, I win; 80 percent of the time, I lose. But I hang in there because I've made contact. I know that fortune favours guts and tenacity. These clients are my neutrals. At any moment, they can turn in my favour—or turn away forever.

The sooner I discern my status with prospects, the more effectively I can invest my time and resources. I walk *away* from detractors. I walk *toward* neutrals. And I *run* toward mobilizers. They are the ones who provide me with the highest ROE: return on energy.

It's not hard to discern the mobilizers. They send all the right messages. They follow through on their promises. They express their gratitude. They treat me like a most-honoured guest.

It's just as easy to discern the detractors. Early on in the process, they reveal their lack of appreciation for my offering.

Their language is dismissive or non-committal. They don't follow through. They make it difficult to work with them. It becomes an exercise in frustration and futility. The neutrals take longer to figure out. They are difficult to read. They don't offer immediate clues. You need to decide how long you engage them before you withdraw. As an optimist, I err on the side of hope and possibility. I go through the motions like I mean it. I lean in until I hit the moment of disconnect. Or I convert them into mobilizers and dance with them from there.

If you're encountering too many detractors and neutrals, it's time to pivot. The market is telling you to change. It's entirely personal and that's how it should be taken. You may need to change your product or your packaging. You may even need to change your market. But you must pay attention to the signals. They will keep getting louder and you'll keep getting angrier.

If you're surrounded by mobilizers, *mazel tov!* You're in the sweet spot. You're doing the right things right. Relish your status. Double down on your efforts. But beware of complacency. Today's rock star is tomorrow's has-been. Mobilizers want to be potentiated. They will run with you for only as long as they believe you will make them faster, stronger, smarter. Then they will migrate to the next Potentiator. Today is a good day to raise your value. Whatever you take for granted, you lose.

The truth is that no matter how awesome you are, you are going to lose your mobilizers sometime soon. We are all in the fashion business. We are hot until we're not. Then it's time to make peace with the passing nature of your appeal and move on: to other people, products or markets.

Play Your Role

No matter who you are, you are playing multiple roles on the different stages of your life: you are a parent, partner, spouse, friend, worker, player, confidante, teacher, student, leader, follower, citizen, disruptor, supporter, innovator, influencer, consumer and producer.

Sometimes, you can play all those roles in a single day. It can be dizzying shape-shifting from one role to the other—literally minute by minute. Certain roles are more comfortable than others. They come easier to us. They align with our natural tendencies. They make us feel in control. They are proof that all is right with the world.

Other roles are much tougher. They don't seem to fit us. We feel false when we play them. They demand qualities that we don't believe we have. They seem to threaten our credibility and reputation. Every time we play them, we're scared we're going to fail. And the most frightening thing of all is that we have to play these roles more often, and there's so much riding on every performance.

You don't need to read this book to discover how you can play your favourite roles well. You're reading this to find out how to play your *toughest* roles with power and poise. These are the roles that you cannot run away from. They are a crucial part of your work, life or play. They determine your ultimate level of success and impact on the lives around you. When you think of them, your pulse accelerates; your palms go sweaty; your chest tightens. You wish you didn't have to play them, but you do. And you have to play them well.

Think about your toughest roles that you have to play. Here are some of mine:

All the world's a stage,
And all the men and
women merely players;
They have their exits
and their entrances;
And one man in his time
plays many parts.

WILLIAM SHAKESPEARE
AS YOU LIKE IT

* Instant guru
* Content champion
* Digital navigator
* Rapid rebounder
* Empowering enabler
* Compassionate coach
* Incessant inspirer
* Compelling communicator

It's in these moments that I need to remember who I am and what I do. As a self-declared Potentiator, I need to play the role of capacity enhancer and power amplifier, no matter what state I'm in. The outside world doesn't care about what's going on inside me. Excepting my immediate family, it's not even relevant to others. The only thing that matters is my utility to the people who have hired me or are considering hiring me. This is easier said than done. That's why there are so few Potentiators. Potentiators understand a fundamental truth: your internal world can be totally disconnected from your external world. As the poet John Milton said, "The mind is its own place, and in it self / Can make a Heav'n of Hell, a Hell of Heav'n." Potentiators know when they're making a hell of heaven. They know the difference between their emotions and their promises. They are able to regulate their performance in the maelstrom.

No matter what the circumstances, you need to play your role if you want to be a Potentiator. Sometimes, you need to consciously act the part, especially when the role is uncustomary for you. Park your feelings of fakeness to the side. Become an **authentic actor**. Yes, it's an oxymoron. You need to express the best part of you while you play your part.

Paradoxically, you can be an even better version of you when you're acting than when you're not.

Many famous players stepped into acting as a way of transcending their limitations. Take Jessica Chastain, the Oscar-nominated actor from such movies as *The Help* and *Zero Dark Thirty*. In 2016, she told James Lipton on *Inside the Actors Studio*: "Acting for me has never been about wanting attention or wanting to be seen . . . it's about connecting with another person and the intimacy of what that is, and so I have to overcome my shyness." Or take Beyoncé, who told *Parade* magazine, "What I feel onstage I don't feel anywhere else. It's an out-of-body experience. I created my stage persona to protect myself so that when I go home I don't have to think about what it is I do."

And in overcoming those limitations, many discover something else. "Acting is not about being someone different," said the legendary Meryl Streep. "It's finding the similarity in what is apparently different, then finding myself in there." For the Potentiator, the challenge is the same: find similarity in difference—and discover your authentic self in the process.

When you're consciously acting, you give yourself licence to explore an expanded persona. You can do and say things that you wouldn't otherwise have dared. At the same time, your assumed identity becomes a second skin that protects you against criticism: it wasn't *you* that people didn't embrace, it was your "act."

The secret to playing your role as the Potentiator is to know how far you can stretch your range. I am a high-energy motivator who needs to thrust myself into presentations in front of hundreds of people. I don't have the luxury of being self-conscious, reserved or reticent. In many instances, I am confronted by a mixture of detractors, mobilizers and neutrals. I am constantly experimenting with new approaches. Sometimes I need to go too far to know how far I can go. That's how I grow. As with anything else, I get better with practice.

MAKE YOUR BREAKTHROUGH

Choose a Role Model

Choose someone who is being the kind of person that you would like to be. Start this week. Study them. Observe their gestures, stance and way of speaking. Listen to their tone, pace and volume. Watch the way they handle difficult moments. See how they recover their composure. And register how they close the sale or clinch the deal. Then emulate them. Incorporate the best part of their style into yours. Absorb their magic and make it your own.

After you've done it once, do it again and again. Be cognizant of the people who are role-modelling excellence, including yourself when you're at your best.

Keep Your Eye on the Path Ahead: Develop Situational Sensibility

Somewhere, someone is already where you want to be. Someone is doing what you want to do and living your dream. They could be just around the corner or just around the world, but they're ahead of your curve. They're the role models you know nothing about. They have all the answers you need—if you only knew who they were.

The secrets to success are hiding in plain sight. They are cloaked in code that is well within your capacity to crack. Everything is clear once it has been seen—but you have to go looking for it. You have to follow the clues wherever they may lead. The most valuable perspectives are ones that you do not currently have. You won't find them in familiar places or comfortable spaces.

Think about your journey so far. Think about the people who have guided you to this point. Think about the teachers, the coaches, the bosses or the artists who have enabled your progress. What is the one thing they all have in common? Situational sensibility—a meta-awareness of an expanded environment, a superior understanding of their domain and a sharpness of vision honed by constant exploration.

Situational sensibility is a full-contact sport. It can be accelerated by book learning but not replaced by it. It demands total immersion in the world that you want to understand. You've got to go deep. Skimming the surface will yield only a superficial view of what's possible.

The 1997 Academy Award–winning movie *Good Will Hunting* is about a 20-year-old janitor called Will Hunting, played by Matt Damon. Hunting is an unrecognized genius, cocky and cynical. As part of a deferred prosecution agreement after assaulting a police officer, he becomes a client of a therapist named Sean Maguire, played by Robin Williams. In a notable scene, Sean tries to communicate the importance of authentic experience and humility to Will.

"So if I asked you about art," Sean says, "you'd probably give me the skinny on every art book ever written. Michelangelo, you know a lot about him. Life's work, political aspirations, him and the pope, sexual orientations, the whole works, right? But I'll bet you can't tell me what it smells like in the Sistine Chapel. You've never actually stood there and looked up at that beautiful ceiling."

Situational sensibility is about reading all about Michelangelo *and* going to the Sistine Chapel. It's about both virtual and physical experience informing and enriching each other. It demands that you get out there, know the trends and connect the dots.

Get Out There—Your Biggest Enemy Is Inertia

Once upon a time, about three thousand years ago, there was a Greek bard called Homer. He wrote about a legendary warrior called Odysseus. Odysseus helped the Greeks win their battle against their archenemies, the Trojans. Then he tried to return home to northwest Greece. It should have been a simple journey; instead, it took him 10 years. He had to fight a giant cyclops and sea monsters, resist the temptations of deadly sirens, fall in love with a witch-goddess and even journey into the underworld to consult with a prophet. But when he returned home, his ordeal wasn't over: he had to engage in a battle to the death with rivals for his wife's affection. Only then could he live "happily ever after."

What's the moral of the story? On your way to "happily ever after," you have to experience the gamut of different phenomena. Some of them may appear strange and scary. Others may seem exciting and exotic. All of them stretch your view of the world—and a mind once stretched can *never* go back to the way it used to be.

It's easier to stay at home where it's safe. It's simpler to bubble yourself in familiar concepts that don't threaten your peace of mind. It's comforting to surround yourself with ideas, people and things that remind you of yourself. It can be disconcerting to discover that there is a better way, or that others are so far ahead of you. It can also be thrilling. It can set you free to dream, dare and do things that would otherwise have been unimaginable. Your nemesis can become your genesis. The dragons that you encounter outside your ramparts enable you to slay the ones within.

If you are the Potentiator, you are an adventurer in a post-Covid world. You have an appetite for new experiences. You crave the epiphanies that accompany being in the physical presence of awesome, big, beautiful, brilliant, inspiring, novel people and things. It's one thing to read about it or watch it on YouTube. It's a totally different thing to see it, touch it, smell it or hear it in real time.

What Would Mandela Do?

Looking back, how many times have your preconceptions of a place or a person been very different from your actual experience of them?

I grew up in Apartheid-era South Africa. For the first 28 years of my life, I lived under a regime that institutionalized racism. As someone who was classified as "white," I benefitted from this regime. I voted for the opposition but I knew it was a sham. I spoke up but not that loudly. Unlike Nelson Mandela,

I saw freedom and justice as principles that I hoped to live for but not principles for which I was prepared to die. Instead, I emigrated to Canada. I took the easy way out because the other path required a toll that I was not prepared to pay.

So Nelson Mandela was both a hero and a rebuke to me. He was an iconic warrior for justice, someone who was prepared to do violence in pursuit of his goals, but also the incarnation of courage and service. I always wanted to meet him but I never thought I would. Then in 2002, out of the blue, I received a request from his foundation to conduct a workshop with their leadership team. My payment was a 15-minute meeting with Nelson Mandela himself.

I expected to be awed and intimidated. Instead, I was so moved that all I could do was cry. It was an out-of-body experience to be comforted by a man who was so sublimely selfless. It gave me a whole new sense of what greatness truly felt like to be around. I had never experienced anything like it before and I haven't since. When I finally composed myself, I asked Mandela a single question: "What was it like suffering for all those years in prison?"

Mandela responded, "I didn't suffer. I prepared to live my life every day so that when I was released, I would transform my nation into the nation I dreamt of it becoming." That statement has impacted my thinking every day since. He intentionally lived his purpose and principles every day, pure and simple. No excuses, alibis or "just-this-times." Whenever I feel a self-pity party coming on, I remember Mandela's words and mood-correct myself. I think WWMD—What Would Mandela Do?—and then I try to do just that.

Pursue the Power of Serendipity—It Only Takes a Small Amount of the Right Insight

Lightning won't strike you if you stay home. You can't collide with opportunity if you don't go anywhere. You won't find flukes under your mattress. Luck is only on the lookout for those who are willing to break their curfews. No matter how gifted you are, without the power of serendipity, you cannot become the Potentiator.

Serendipity is when great things, people or chances bump into you because you're in the right place at the right time. You attend an industry conference and you meet someone who needs exactly what you have to sell. You participate in a continuing education program and you learn the one thing that helps everything else make sense. You volunteer for a charity event and connect with someone who offers you the job of a lifetime or becomes your life partner. You travel somewhere that you've never been before and discover an extraordinary investment opportunity. You make a new friend who introduces you to a whole new community.

Serendipity is the reward for taking action. It's a kind of everyday lottery that transforms your life—by a little or by a lot. When you are the Potentiator, you are a serendipity magnet because you are constantly thrusting yourself into situations where you're likely to be lucky. Just as 50 percent of all pregnancies are unplanned, at least half of our good fortune is serendipitous. What's more, the more you believe in serendipity, the more it becomes a self-fulfilling prophecy. If you believe it, and do everything to attract it, it will come.

There will be days when you lose your passion for the game. You don't feel like venturing beyond your comfort zone.

Serendipity is the reward for taking action.

―――――――

It takes all you have just to keep up with the losers. Those are the days when you need to remind yourself to get out there. It's called *conditioning*. Serendipity doesn't run on your schedule. The day you stay home is the day your destiny shows up at the place you didn't visit. Remember: if you don't feel ready to rumble, act as though you do. You'll be surprised by how emotion flows from motion.

Context is Decisive: Know the Trends

The key to situational sensibility is understanding the context in which you are operating. *Context* is defined as the circumstances that form the setting for an event, statement or idea, and in terms of which it can be fully understood. It's the 360-degree view of your situation that enables you to approach it from multiple angles. It's also your ability to articulate your vision in a way that others can easily understand. You know that you know the trends only when you can help others know the trends. That's why I'm writing this book. That's why I'm sharing my point of view as often as I can. Every conversation is a test of my ability to convey actionable insights that potentiate other people's success.

If you master your situational sensibility, you'll always be in an empowered state. You'll act from a place of strength, not panic. You'll know what to do and how to do it, even if you have to pivot later. Everything will occur to you as an opening for action, not a threat of shutdown. The irony is that it's always easier to change before circumstances force you to change, although we often change only when we have no other choice but to change. By then, it's always much more difficult.

According to the Environics 2021 Social Values Study, fewer than half of North Americans report that they are adapting to waves of complexity and uncertainty in a post-Covid reality. The majority of people are uncomfortable with change. So as the Potentiator, you are also a comfort provider. You make it safe for people to go where they've never been before.

Post-Covid Onset: Adaptability in the U.S. & Canada
(% reporting statement reflects their opinion fairly well or exactly)

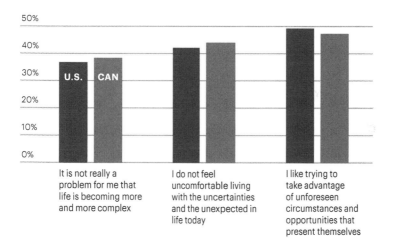

SOURCE: *Environics US Social Values Survey, 2020; Environics Canadian Social Values Survey, 2021 (© 2021 Environics Research, all rights reserved)*

As a result of my research and everyday conversations with a vast range of people, I have identified eight trends that are transforming the future. They are simple and powerful. As I walk you through them, think about how they're impacting your world. Think about whether you're anticipating them or reacting to them.

1 **Personal wellness: from sidebar to main thing.** The opposite of *wellness* is not disease. It's *ignorance*. Ignorance isn't bliss; it can be fatal. Covid elevated self-care to the top of all our agendas. "Staying safe" now means protection against disease and dis-ease. Prior to Covid, the majority of people treated their personal wellbeing as an afterthought. Now wellness is the number one issue because it drives the success of everything else. As the Potentiator, you must take great care of yourself so you can take great care of others.

2 **Life integration: the merging of home and office.** We're working where we live and living where we work. All separation is futile. Being able to navigate the new professional realm means mentally commuting while you switch rooms. The office is where you go to physically meet people so you can brainstorm and bond. Home is where you do the work that can be done solo or online. As the Potentiator, you must demonstrate professional ambidexterity.

3 **Avatar evolution: mastering hybrid communication.** No matter what comes next, online will coexist with in-person. We're all part avatar, part flesh and blood. Being able to toggle back and forth effectively between physical and virtual communication will be a core capability. It's not good enough just being good enough. You have to be great on Teams, Zoom or WebEx. Every conversation will become more valuable in the face of everything else competing for people's attention. As the Potentiator, you must inhabit the avatar that best expresses your true self.

4 **Everyday activism: the rise of ESG.** It's not just about doing things right; it's about doing the right things.

Environmental, social and governance (ESG) considerations are dictating how and where resources are being invested. We're voting with our attention, time and dollars. Stewardship, social justice and ethical leadership are everybody's business. They must permeate your language and guide your actions. As the Potentiator, you must be seen to walk the ESG talk.

5 **Earned trust: the drive for dependability.** In the maelstrom of continuous, cataclysmic change, we crave the familiar. In the face of gargantuan challenges, we want trusted champions by our side. We turn to people and brands that have proved their dependability. We seek the comfort of confidantes who have come through for us in the crunch moments. Our greatest resource is go-to people who will help us raise our game. As the Potentiator, your every action must build other people's belief in you.

6 **Moonshot mindset: the outsizing of ambition.** In the wake of Covid, there's been an explosion of innovation and breakthroughs in almost every sector of our economy. From financial services to healthcare to entertainment to government, the notion of impossible has been totally redefined. Along with great misery came some great miracles. If you can dream it, you can do it faster and smarter than ever before. As the Potentiator, you must create by example.

7 **Collective connection: it takes a global village.** Nothing brings people together like an unprecedented pandemic. It's a universal experience that instantly establishes common ground. It sparks curiosity about how others are handling it and compassion for the toll it has taken. It's

the first thing we want to know when we meet. It also motivates each of us to share more of ourselves than we ever would have previously. Zoom has brought us into people's homes and offered a window into their personal lives. We're being enriched by each other's perspective. As the Potentiator, you must create an exchange that enables others to grow.

8 **Personal accountability: it's up to you, along with everyone else.** Covid set in motion a 21st-century renaissance that is inviting each of us to reexamine our contribution. Automatic pilot is not an option. Neither is withdrawal, resignation or abdication. Just standing on the sidelines or bellowing from the bleachers won't make the difference others are counting on you to deliver. Every person matters. As the Potentiator, you must inspire others by playing your role the best way you can.

If you don't have an opinion about the eight trends above, remember that disruption begins long before you feel its consequences. Inaction will turn you into a *disruptee*: someone who procrastinated *too long* and paid *too high* a price for it. The common (and urgent) thread with each of these trends? The need to go first—and to fully understand your business environment.

Imagine if you could have a drone flying 1,000 feet above you, sending you images of what was happening all around you. Better yet, imagine if this drone could send you images of what was *about to happen*. Imagine if, like Google Maps or Waze, it could warn you of blockages, backups or breakdowns along the way—and suggest alternate routes. That's what understanding the transformative trends allows: it can show what you need to do *now* in order to win *later*.

MAKE YOUR BREAKTHROUGH

Get Hip to the Transformative Trends that Will Get You in the Game

Make a list of five transformative trends that you are observing. Identify how they are transforming and disrupting your world. Share them with your peers and ask them for their ideas. Get their feedback on how you can use each one to succeed and potentiate others. Make a list of three things you'll need to change for each one. Have some fun with this assignment. You can even stage a trend party where people come dressed as a transformative trend.

What Are You Telling the World?
Make a Powerful Promise

By now, you're self-savvy and situationally sensible. You know yourself and your environment. You're a student of context and the possibilities it creates. But do you know your purpose and can you declare it to others? Do you have a specific value proposition that you can express with clarity and conviction? And are you executing your value proposition with focus?

The answers to those questions point to the difference between sharp and vague, crucial and incidental, fulfilled and

Safe doesn't live here anymore and it's never coming back.

frustrated. The world is full of people who don't know where they're going. They *sort of*, *kind of* know. They are moving in the general direction of their desires. They're achieving a moderate level of success. They work hard. They follow the rules. Their life is good because "good enough" is good enough for them. And that's okay. There is no judgement in these words. Holding on to the safety rails is a prudent way to live.

When you're the Potentiator, however, you're out to achieve something *big*. You want to impact other people's lives and make a meaningful difference. You think beyond yourself and your immediate realities—and you see possibilities that excite you. You plan your execution and execute your plan. You run toward the toughest problems because that's where the richest opportunities are hiding.

A promise is something that you make with your mouth. It's a declaration that assures others something will happen because you say so. It's only as good as the person who makes it. The most trustful question we can ever ask is, "You promise?" We want to believe in the integrity of others. We want to rely on them to pull us through. We want their talent to work on our behalf. We want to be inspired and empowered in equal measure.

I would like to slay a sacred cow right here: don't under-promise and over-deliver. That is a formula for mediocrity. It means you're setting the other person's sights low so that you can exceed them. You're building in slack as a buffer for low performance. You're indulging in your own fear of disappointing yourself and others. You're putting yourself first by protecting yourself against failure. Simply stated, you're playing it safe. But safe doesn't live here anymore and it's never coming back. There is no comfortable way to be great and there is no great way to be comfortable.

There is another risk to under-promising: your customers, clients or prospects could be underwhelmed by your offering. They may not have the patience or the inclination to wait for your actions to speak for you. They don't want just satisfactory. They want legendary, superb, fabulous, extraordinary, amazing, sets-new-standards, thrilled—no matter what discipline you're in. Awesome is the new standard practice.

But the opposite of under-promising isn't over-promising. Over-promising is lying. It's a dishonest attempt to win someone's trust or support by exaggerating the benefit you can deliver to them. It's the currency of con men, an abuse of good faith that will incur the wrath of your victims and inevitable personal misfortune. You can fool a smart person only once. And even one time is too many. In the age of digital likes and dislikes, your reputation always precedes you. What happens in Vegas stays on YouTube.

The opposite of under-promising is making a **powerful promise**. This means making a promise that captivates others and enrols them in your cause. It is ambitious and audacious. It stretches your capacity. It pushes your envelope. It even scares you. You know that it's going to take everything you have to actualize your commitment. But you also know that you will grow in direct proportion to its size. It's nowhere near an over-promise because you know you'll do whatever it takes to make it real.

The tension between who you are now and who you have to become to make good on your powerful promise is what makes you the Potentiator. You're the best example of why people should believe in you.

This entire book is my powerful promise to you. I'm making a big bet on my ability to substantiate my declaration. I'm playing as big as I dare to play while I transfer my insights to you. Every word is a deposit on my claim. The fact that you're reading this is proof that I'm coming through for you. And we're just getting started.

Don't undermine your contribution so other factors take precedence. In a world of multi-causation, ensure that others assign a higher value to your contribution. Augment the attribution that they assign to your role in their success. Don't overinvest in your personal significance, but don't discount it either. Frame your contribution in a way that makes people want to experience it for real—at the expense of your competition.

Often, the hardest part of any assignment is winning it. Before you can show how good you are, you have to earn the right to do it. If others haven't worked with you before, they have to trust an impression of you formed by your communication and your reputation. Robert Cialdini, the renowned "godfather of influence," coined the term **pre-suasion**. This is the ability to move people in a direction that persuades them to give assent to a message before they encounter it. It earns their attention and channels their focus in a way that makes the message more likely to be successful.

Think about meeting someone who has been described as having "a magic touch" or being "absolutely brilliant" or being "the ultimate professional." How would you feel just before the meeting? What would your expectations be? That's what we're talking about here: creating the perception that you want others to have of you and then living it.

Being the Potentiator means being willing to promote yourself so you can promote others. I make a living by being a great pre-suader. Unless I can shape other people's opinions of me, I cannot practice my craft. The way into the boardroom is by invitation only. Kudos and cachet are my passports to the centres of power and influence. Then all I have to do is keep raising the bar. Momentum builds momentum—so long as I continue to increase the success of the people I serve.

There are four essential elements to making a powerful promise:

1 Declare your purpose
2 Keep your eyes on the prize
3 Express your value proposition
4 Focus your execution

1 Declare Your Purpose

How badly do you want it? What price are you willing to pay to make it real? What dragons are you prepared to slay to rescue it? Why are you willing to give your all every day?

Purpose is the rocket fuel of Potentiators. It is the conscious reason why they exist and why they do what they do. It is both a dream and a mission. It's the source of their determination and inspiration.

If your purpose is strong enough, you'll transcend any obstacle in front of you. Walls are there to keep uncommitted people out. The totally committed ones will find a way under, over, around or through. They will also clear the path for others to follow.

Your purpose is the intersection of three forces:

What you love to do—if you don't love it, you won't stick with it.

What you are great at doing—if you're not great at it, you won't make others great.

What you want to achieve—if you don't know your prize, you won't pull others toward it.

When Jeff Bezos founded Amazon, he wanted to create "earth's most customer-centric company; to build a place where people can come to find and discover anything they might want to buy online."

When Larry Page and Serge Brin founded Google, they wanted "to organize the world's information and make it universally accessible and useful."

Walt Disney's purpose was "to create happiness."

Mike Lipkin's purpose is to feed people's confidence and excite them into action.

MAKE YOUR BREAKTHROUGH

Define Your Purpose

What's your purpose? What makes you dance, laugh, cry, exult, celebrate, soar? What can you dedicate your life to achieving? How can you enable others to fully self-actualize? Begin by writing your responses to the three forces:

1 What do you love to do?
2 What are you great at doing?
3 What do you want to achieve?

Distill your responses into a single statement. Have some fun with it. Fine-tune it. Get some feedback. Version 1.0 is never perfect.

Once you've defined your purpose, you need to declare it. When you declare something, you announce it publicly. You make it official. You own it. You are willing to be judged by it. You're accountable for it. You're disciplined by it. You have to take the actions commensurate with it. You have a built-in focus that cuts through distraction and spotlights opportunity.

In *every* meeting, declare your purpose to your clients or customers. No matter what company you represent, you represent yourself first. Give others a reason to believe in you. Then strengthen that belief. Remind people why you are "the one" for the role or assignment over and over again. It never gets tired if you never get tired.

2 Keep Your Eyes On the Prize

There's no point in competing if you're not competing for a highly desirable prize. A prize is defined as reward and recognition for an outstanding achievement. It's an ambition that thrills you every time you think about it. It's the image of fulfillment that makes the struggle worthwhile. Every time you see it, you're motivated to stretch a little further.

The beauty of the prize is that you decide how often you choose to look at it. Non-Potentiators forget about their prize.

They're mired in their minutiae and fettered by their frustrations. As the Potentiator, on the other hand, you keep your prize front and centre all the time. That's how you sustain your remarkable performance. You see yourself winning the prize in advance, so you're in constant lag time—in your mind, you've already won. The work required to turn it into reality is just a formality.

For me, visualizing this book in the hands of 100,000 readers is my prize. That's what electrifies me. Early on in this process, I commissioned the design of the front cover so I could literally see it in front of me. Then I populated the pages with these words, hour by hour, day by day, week by week until I crossed the finish line.

MAKE YOUR BREAKTHROUGH

Name Your Prize

Write down your prize that makes all the blood, sweat and tears worth it. Express it in a way that makes it bigger than any barriers getting in the way of it. Visualize yourself achieving it. Write down how that would make you feel.

---

3 Express Your Value Proposition

If your purpose is the reason why you exist and do what you do, your value proposition is how you persuade others to buy or use it. It's the secret sauce that makes it unique and irresistible. It's how you bring it alive and whet others' appetite for more. It's the recipe for monetizing or commercializing your purpose in a way that cannot be matched by anyone else.

When a celebrity chef like Nigella Lawson or Jamie Oliver walks you through the way they make an omelette or a steak, they put their unique stamp on their creations. An omelette or a steak is a staple meal—but not in their hands. They transform it through their narrative and personal spice.

Lawson and Oliver are culinary performers. Their entire professional existence is a function of their ability to captivate viewers and encourage others to try their recipes. The food is just the raw material of their powerful promise. Their value proposition is the cachet they create around each recipe and how that cachet attaches itself to you when you prepare the same meal.

You may be a scientist, a salesperson, an actuary or an accountant. You may be designing a product or service that is similar to thousands of other offerings. The offering doesn't matter as much as the way *you* offer it. Obviously, it must deliver at an expected level—but the differentiator is *you*.

There is a French phrase that has been integrated into English: *je ne sais quoi*. It literally means "I don't know what." It is used to describe something attractive, distinctive or special about someone that is hard to put into words. That's why people have difficulty defining their personal *je ne sais quoi*. But define it you must. Otherwise you cannot live it.

Leading consumer brands invest thousands of hours and billions of dollars labelling their products and services as indispensable to our lifestyles. Each one of us needs to invest the personal equivalent labelling our crucial contribution to our stakeholders. Here are seven examples of what the world's leading brands present as their value propositions:

Separate the person you are from the brand that the person represents.

- **Apple Watch:** If you wear an Apple Watch, you will look smart, be healthy and stay connected.

- **Tesla Model S:** If you drive a Tesla Model S, you will brand yourself as someone on the cutting edge of change and style while you experience industry-defining, *clean* performance.

- **Canada Goose Snow Mantra Parka:** If you wear a Canada Goose Snow Mantra Parka, you will be fashionable while you protect yourself against the cold with an authentic parka that is field-tested at the earth's lowest temperatures.

- **Red Bull:** If you drink Red Bull Energy Drink, you will have unique energy or *wings* whenever you need them.

- **Johnnie Walker Black Label Whisky:** If you drink Johnnie Walker Black Label, you will be recognized as someone who appreciates the finer things in life while you enjoy its legendary Scottish heritage.

- **Rolex Sea-Dweller:** If you own a Rolex Sea-Dweller, you will be seen as the sort of person who is rich, professional and prepared for extreme adventure and exploration—even if you never leave the city.

- **Visa:** If you use Visa, you have the security and convenience of using the world's most widely used way to pay for anything.

You are a brand just like any of these icons. Separate the person you are from the brand that the person represents. For example, there is a Mike Lipkin who has a family, two dogs and a house in Toronto. He works as a motivator, coach and researcher. He likes to travel and listen to fiction audiobooks.

But there is also the global brand called Mike Lipkin. He is the Potentiator. He expands people's capacity to produce remarkable results through insights and inspiration, which enable them to play at their best. They do things they never would have done as a result of their association with him.

Mike Lipkin, the person, isn't shy about telling you about Mike Lipkin, the brand. The person depends on the brand for a living. He has to champion the brand so that he can get a chance to show how powerful the brand is. Then, he relies on his work to turn his clients into advocates and influencers.

Mike's value proposition is that he will give you the insights and inspiration to do things you never would have done—and to realize results you never would have achieved. He will nudge, cajole, coach, push, stretch and "do whatever it takes" to help you live your dream.

MAKE YOUR BREAKTHROUGH

Create Your Value Proposition— and Send It to Me

Write down your value proposition. Include these three elements:

1 It must communicate the special impact you have on others.

2 It must leverage your core expertise or skills.

3 It must call other people into action.

Have some fun with it. Share it with friends, colleagues and confidantes. Get feedback, then fine-tune it. Then seize every opportunity to express it. I'm also interested to see it. Send it to me at mike.lipkin@ environics.ca.

4 Focus Your Execution

Distraction is like death by a thousand cuts. There is always a reason to do something else instead of the thing that you know you must do. The easy way out always seems more attractive than the hard way in. Procrastination is an addictive opioid. The ping of a text or incoming email is an irresistible invitation to anesthetize oneself against the pain of intense effort or fear of unfamiliar actions. But the pain of regret expands in direct proportion to the degree of distraction.

Focus is the Potentiator's DNA. It is the capacity to concentrate on what really matters, no matter what the circumstances. It is the one thing that is within everyone's control. Right now, I'm concentrating on creating these words. There is noise swirling around me. There are literally hundreds of other things that I could be doing. But none of those other things will help this book materialize. I've chosen to focus on this activity to the exclusion of all else in *this* moment.

Making anything great is never easy. The bigger your ambition, the harder the task. Focus lets you see things that you would otherwise miss. It takes time. You can look at something for minutes or hours or days without identifying the breakthrough you need. The irony is that epiphanies are the fruit of prolonged focus. The longer we sit and think, the more tempted we are to distract ourselves. But the more tempted we are to distract ourselves, the more we need to focus. Winners are often the people who can sit with a problem the longest.

I have sat with this book for over two years while I adapted to a post-Covid reality. I purposefully blocked out the time to focus on the project while I culled non-essential work. I planned the meetings, transcribed the notes, did the research, consulted my networks, went back to the drawing board, partnered with the publishers, endured the frustrations, rolled with the setbacks and eventually sent the manuscript to the printers. Voilà, here we are! Things only look easy when you don't know the backstory.

You can immediately tell the difference between something that is done with focus and something that is produced with part-time attention. It's in every detail. Focus is captivating. Lack of focus is annoying. Focus is the greatest gift we can give anyone. It says: they are the centres of our universe; nothing is more important than their joy or satisfaction. But you cannot give what you do not have. Without personal focus, it's impossible to focus on others.

MAKE YOUR BREAKTHROUGH

Five Actions to Focus Your Execution

Make a commitment to getting results with these five simple actions. You can do some of them right now. You can definitely do all of them in the next week. They're easy to understand but not always easy to do. So invest the time and effort. Your return will be remarkable.

1 **Make an appointment with your own priorities.** Remember your purpose. Declare it over and over again. Be mindful of your value proposition. Then live it. We all have to manage minutiae. That's table stakes. Potentiators do more of the major things. "I'm too busy" or "I just don't have the time" are the lamentations of losers.

2 **Focus entirely on what you're doing while you're doing it.** Practice your focus and focus your practice. There will be inevitable interruptions that you cannot control, but learn to control the ones that you can.

3 **When you're with others, focus only on them.** In the digital age, physical presence is sacrosanct. Turn the phone off or place it face down so you cannot be distracted by a text that cannibalizes your connection.

4 **Have regular check-ins with yourself and others.** Ask the question, "How could I have done this

better?" Be gentle on yourself when you mess up the first time, even if you mess up the same way a second time. But not the third time.

5 **Communicate your contributions.** Humble-brag if you have to. Don't assume that people always appreciate your role in their success. Be creative in the way you help others appreciate your value to them.

2

The Second Potentiator Practice
Build Robust Resilience

They tried to bury us. They didn't know we were seeds.

MEXICAN PROVERB

I N PHYSICS, resilience is the ability of an elastic material (such as rubber or animal tissue) to absorb energy (such as from a blow) and release that energy back to its original shape. The word *resilience* derives from the Latin verb *resilire*, meaning "to jump back."

The more elastic the material, the greater its ability to absorb and release energy. In human terms, the more robust someone is, the more they are able to recover their original shape or spirit. *Robust* means strong, healthy and vigorous. It defines the kind of post-Covid resilience that is required to jump back from a series of apocalyptic blows. It's not just a passive capacity to endure setbacks or losses; it's an active skill that can be strengthened with practice and awareness.

The truth is that some people are naturally more resilient than others: they are wired to withstand adversity. It may be their nature or it may be the way they were nurtured. They're empowered with a magical ability to thrive on adversity—just as a chess prodigy anticipates the perfect move, or a math genius can solve the unsolvable problem.

I am not one of those people.

I am not naturally resilient. However, I am becoming *robustly resilient* as a result of this work. Throughout my life, I have wrestled with depression. I have been so far down that even down looked up. I have undergone cognitive, pharmacological and electroconvulsive therapy. My wings have been broken so many times that they've formed a whole new shape, which enables me to fly.

I tell people that I'm so motivated because I attend my own seminars. That's not a joke. It's an acute consciousness that I continuously activate. The alternative is the temptation to *catastrophize*: to see every negative event as a potential existential threat. The wolf is always at the door—even if I am the only one who can see it.

And I know that, just like me, you have your own demons to deal with.

This chapter will empower you to revel in a post-Covid reality. It will introduce you to a set of tools that you can use to excel in your forthcoming crises. It won't make them easier; you'll still need to sweat, struggle and even cry your way through them. But you will become better at resolving them and turning them into breakthrough moments.

Swim Toward the Wave

Robust resilience is adaptive and anticipatory. Surfers—masters of the ultimate socially distanced sport—are the perfect exemplars of robust resilience. They don their wetsuits, get on their boards and swim out to meet the perfect wave. Then they spend hours sitting on their boards as they scan the horizon for the next wave. When they think they see it, they move toward it. Then they paddle as fast as they can to catch it. Sometimes they succeed. Most times they don't. It doesn't matter to them. Being in the water is a highly desirable pursuit all by itself. Waiting and watching are as much a part of the endeavour as slicing down the wave at 15 to 30 kilometres per hour. In any two-to-three-hour session, even a good surfer will catch only six to nine waves. Each "rip" (excellent surf) will last only a few seconds. But even one rip is worth the entire effort. Surfers reflect their passion for the sport. Whether they are world class or amateur aficionados, they look like they are robust.

Big-wave surfers also train themselves to hold their breath when they are held down by the water. Even if they're held under for a few seconds, their natural instinct is to panic. Breath-hold training teaches that the mind plays a major role. Thinking uses oxygen. Panic and struggling burn it fast. The key is to keep calm and relax, just like in a pandemic. Resilience and panic are mutually exclusive.

According to a 2018 article by Luke Gartside in *Wavelength* magazine, very few people actually drown while surfing. Out of an estimated population of 23 million surfers globally, there are approximately 10 fatalities per year—on par with long-distance running. The point is that the panic is out of all proportion to reality. It's the big lie that masquerades as the temporary truth in your mind. Know that this horrible moment will pass—and you will live to catch many more rips.

Ultimately, you must thrust yourself into situations that will test you to the max. Put yourself at the mercy of the waves. If you're out to do something great, get ready to encounter

Winners will always lose more because they are trying new things.

crushing rejections and devastating defeats. When you're ambitious and passionate, every setback feels bigger than it is. That's because you care disproportionately about the outcome. It's both the upside and the downside of being crazy about your cause.

Learn to Be Disappointed, Not Destroyed

At the 2018 Winter Olympics in PyeongChang, South Korea, 2,833 athletes competed; only 103 gold medals were won. There was near certainty that loss would plague even the best competitors. Winning is sweet but losing is inevitable. Still, there is a big difference between being disappointed and being destroyed. Disappointment is a passing sense of unhappiness or displeasure because you didn't achieve your goal; destruction is an emotional implosion that cripples you from competing at the highest level.

Everybody loves to win; very few people are prepared to lose. That doesn't just mean you know there is a possibility of losing. It means that you are ready to lose. You are even great at losing. Winners will always lose more because they are trying new things. They are competing in more games. They're asking for more orders. They're thrusting themselves into situations that more timid souls would never explore. By definition, therefore, winners need to be losers. As the novelist George Moore said, "A winner is a just a loser who tried one more time."

You cannot give what you do not have; you cannot share where you haven't been. If you're going to cause breakthroughs with others, you need to demonstrate your capacity to stay the course. You need the scars that come with getting into tough scrapes. Past failures are the teachers that enable you to educate others. The best role models parade their imperfections. They transform others' views of what's possible through their transparency and authenticity.

As the Potentiator, I guarantee you that, at some point, you will have to cause breakthroughs with others while you're under attack or weathering adversity. Other people's success doesn't conform to your agenda or align with your peace of mind. That's when you need robust resilience to power you through the rough patches.

You've got to roll with your emotions while you move relentlessly forward. If you can handle the depths, you can rise to the heights. You can't have one without the other.

MAKE YOUR BREAKTHROUGH

Focus on Your Failures

Write down your three biggest failures and the biggest lesson that you learned from each of them. In the next few weeks, when you're talking with someone who needs a breakthrough, share the lessons you've learned to help the other person see their setback or failure as a resource that they can draw on to achieve future success.

It Takes a Village

Robust resilience is a team sport. All the available social research shows that building strong relationships builds robust resilience. The more people on your team, the greater your psychological wellbeing. You can face the future only because of the people who have your back. We're all angels with one wing: we can fly only by embracing each other.

Investing in relationships is the best insurance you can have for the adversity and crises that are part of everyone's future. The most pleasurable parts of my days are the invigorating conversations I have with outstanding colleagues, clients, confidantes and collaborators. That's how I fill my intellectual and emotional tanks. In turn, I have to fill other people's tanks.

If you're not having fun while you're connecting with others, you're not doing it right. Unless you derive a deep delight from conversations, you won't make it a pleasure for others. They must look forward to their calls with you, especially if they're virtual. Here are my questions: Would you want to talk with you? Would you want to invest more time with you? Would you feel more resilient as a result of talking with you? Are you a net gain? Or a net pain?

As the neuroscientist David Eagleman has said, "Normal brain function depends on the social web around us. Our neurons require other people's neurons to thrive and survive." Every brain is a network of networks. There's no such thing as a robustly resilient loner. We're only as good as the company we keep. And we only keep the company that we constantly earn.

Inside every Potentiator is someone who needs help as much as the people they are helping. Superman has Clark Kent. Spider-Man has Peter Parker. Batman has Bruce Wayne. Wonder Woman has Diana Prince. The Hulk has Bruce Banner. I have the versions of myself that only my family, best friends, coaches or therapists see. That's when I can shed my superhero persona and show my vulnerability. I can get lost and confused, or be helpless and hesitant. I can be the guided, not the guide. That's the power of coaches and confidantes. They enable us to step back so we can also step up. There is no other way to sustain one's intensity in the service of others.

Interpret to Win through Robust Resilience Responses

No one goes through life unscathed. When the rain falls, it falls on everyone. At some point, we will all take an eight count. Life is about losing things. Love hurts. People leave. Friends become frenemies. Our health ebbs and flows. We'll be hired and fired. Our finances will go up and then they'll go down. The wrong side often wins.

Why do some people become better while others become bitter? What's the difference between those who thrive on rejection and those who submit to dejection? Is there an epiphany that separates those-who-find-a-way from those-who-fade-away?

The answer is yes. It's not our experiences themselves that make us happy or miserable; it's the meaning we attach to them that does. It's not what happens that influences us; it's how we interpret what happens. We're only as happy as the stories we tell ourselves.

Our instinctive response may not always be the best response because it's based on past paradigms or experience. Sometimes it serves us and sometimes it doesn't. Think about how you would interpret the following scenarios. Then review the Robust Resilience Response (RRR) for each one that empowers you to carry on—with even greater vigour and enthusiasm:

1 Your client or colleague gets angry with you. They raise their voice. They reprimand you in front of others.

Your instinctive response may be to shout or snap back.

RRR: Although you are surprised by the other person, you retain your composure. You let them know their behaviour is inappropriate to the situation. You state that you wish to resolve the issue offline. Even though you may feel enraged, you respond with grace and poise.

2 You discover that a major account has been awarded to the competition despite your client having just praised you for the value you've brought to their business.

Your instinctive response may be to express shock, confusion and personal doubt.

RRR: You allow yourself to experience disappointment for an hour. You vent with confidantes. You go for a walk and curse no one in particular. Then you get back to work. You call the client to learn why you lost their business.

3 You make a presentation at a marquee meeting that falls flat. You receive feedback that confirms your lack of impact.

Your instinctive response may be to brand yourself as a poor communicator and lose your confidence. You may even be hesitant to get in front of the client again.

RRR: You allow yourself to wrestle with discomfort. You replay the agony of the presentation in your mind for the rest of the day. You seek guidance from your allies or supporters in the audience. Then you evaluate each aspect of your presentation and find ways to improve it. You plan your next presentation as soon as possible.

4 You expect a promotion that has been promised to you. But the person who made the promise leaves the company. The promotion goes to someone else.

Your instinctive response may be to see the universe as biased against you and to lose faith in positive outcomes. You are tempted to become cynical and skeptical.

RRR: You allow yourself to be angry or upset for a week, although you don't publicly exhibit your emotions. Then you accept the decision and choose whether to stay or leave. If you stay, you act like you voted for the person who received the promotion. If you leave, you don't look back in resentment. You expect another opportunity to present itself soon and you act accordingly.

5 **You make an investment that goes sour. As a result, you lose thousands of dollars.**

Your instinctive response may be to panic and worry that you have a reverse Midas touch. You start to doubt all your other investments. You second-guess your next move.

RRR: You lament your loss for a week. You uncover exactly what happened. You decide to continue the relationship with your advisor or to sever it. You seek professional guidance on how to avoid similar misfortune in the future. Then you move on. You understand that money isn't personal. It can come or go at any time.

6 **You set yourself an important goal that you believe you can achieve. You tell many people that you will achieve it. But you don't.**

Your instinctive response may be embarrassment or shame. You may even try to hide the outcome. You resolve never to declare your ambition again. You decide to shrink your ambition.

RRR: You explore why you didn't achieve your goal. You set a new one. You don't worry what other people think. You know they probably don't even remember your goal in the first place. Those who matter won't care; those who care won't matter. You don't shrink your goal—you expand your efforts.

7 You hear that an influential person in your work environment has derided you. You believe it can negatively impact your career.

Your instinctive response may be to obsess about the reasons why this person did it or be disturbed by their detractive comments. You're confused as to why they would even say those things about you. You're unable to shed the feelings of anger or indignation.

RRR: You allow yourself to experience the shock of disbelief or indignation. Then you bring your emotions under control. You seek other points of view about what was really communicated. You plan how you will approach this person to get them to cease their comments and even redress the situation. Then you take action. In the meantime, you focus on all the people who are championing your cause.

8 Someone you trust makes a big promise to you. They don't follow through on it. And they don't even apologize.

Your instinctive response may be to become embittered or estranged from that person. You feel betrayed. You even feel stupid for believing in them in the first place.

RRR: You allow yourself to feel hurt for a day or a week, depending on the impact of the broken promise. You find out why they didn't follow through. You choose whether to call them on it or simply walk away. You also choose whether to give them another chance or sever ties. Whatever you decide, you forgive them for their actions. You let go of your anger for your own peace of mind. You feel wiser not exploited.

⑨ Someone you love or care deeply about decides to end their relationship with you.

Your instinctive response may be to collapse in heartbreak and blame. You resolve never to be vulnerable again. You brand the world as cruel and unfair.

RRR: You allow yourself to experience pain for as long as it takes for the pain to subside. You accept the other person's decision. You learn why they left you. You choose to change your ways or simply decide that the relationship has run its course. You don't shut down; you stay vulnerable, open and loving. You know that your next soulmate is just around the corner.

⑩ You're working on an assignment that could represent a breakthrough for you, but you're not succeeding in enlisting your clients and colleagues to your cause. You feel like your efforts are futile.

Your instinctive response may be to give up on your goals. You resign yourself to failure. You feel impotent because you can't forward the action. You lose your optimism about your ability to influence the future.

RRR: You allow yourself to feel the frustration and angst at not being able to achieve your desired outcomes. Then you review your strategy. You interview your stakeholders to find out why they're unresponsive. You ideate new approaches with your team and other members of your network. You take total accountability for finding a new way to a win-win situation.

These are 10 common scenarios that are part of life's everyday drama. I have given you my Robust Resilience Responses; you may have a different way of dealing with them. The most important robust resilience mantra is this: "Discover for yourself." Without discovery, there is no mastery. Own your response, whatever it is. Robust resilience means never blaming anyone or anything else for your challenges. The response-ability is always your own.

When we change our minds, the world doesn't change but we live in a new world. The moment that you intentionally interpret everything like the Potentiator, you engage life on new terms. Everything becomes a means to an end: helping others play at their best. For better or for worse, in sickness and in health, you bring the weather. You become a not-so-secret agent of success. You make sense of things that don't make sense for others. That's why they will be drawn to you.

Nothing that I'm sharing with you is meant for extraordinary intellects. Ordinary people can be the Potentiator. It's the way that you interact with life that makes you extraordinary. You screen out the disablers and the detractors. When you're the Potentiator, you're not blind to the danger or downside. But you're also not distracted by them. I call it "dynamic deniability."

Dynamic deniability is the refusal to grant disempowering things the power to ambush your wellbeing or positivity. For example, I know that millions of people have been traumatized by the impact of the pandemic. Instead of being depressed by this thought, I'm inspired by the possibility of helping them. I'm also immensely grateful for the culture in which we live and the extraordinary opportunities that have opened up for me.

MAKE YOUR BREAKTHROUGH

Catch People When They Are Interpreting to Win

Over the next week, observe the people around you. Distinguish those who are "interpreting to win." Discern their words and actions. Tell them that you're impressed by their responses. Communicate the lessons that you've learned from them. Ask them for their perspective. At first, they may be astonished by your comments. But then they will share a gem that enriches your capacity to make an even greater difference. However they respond, they will be delighted with the recognition. They will also be aware of their Potentiator qualities in a way that they weren't before. Then they will pay it forward.

Go for No

While you can control your response to situations, you can't control how people respond or react to you. Sometimes—many times—you might get a "no," "no thanks" or "not interested" when you put yourself or your ideas on the line.

And guess what? That can be the best thing to happen to you. Pursue every opportunity to hear the word no. Thrust yourself into impossible situations. Take chances when the odds are stacked against you. Do what you've never done before. Call people you've never called before. Make promises you've never made before. Say what you've never said before. Motivate other people to say, "No, not now, not yet, not ever." Give yourself a wake-up call so you can awaken the power within others.

Every time you hear no, you grow. You come face-to-face with your fear. You stare it in the eyes and you don't blink. You take pride in your courage and commitment to your cause. You smile because you've taken control. You've dared where others were afraid to tread. You've strengthened your mental muscles to go for even more nos. Champions will always collect more nos than anyone else. They are trying more things. They are risking more personal capital. They are learning more techniques. They are experimenting with new approaches. They are setting themselves up for success.

Think about your breakthrough moments. Sometimes they were highly pleasurable, and sometimes they were acutely painful—but either way, they accelerated your evolution to the next level. But don't wait for others to move you into action. Make your *own* breakthroughs by surprising others. One of the best things you can say is, "Wow, I've never done that before. I'm amazed at myself. Phew."

When you hear the word no, it means that you've asked for something. You've made a request. You've elicited a response. You've got onto someone else's radar. You've planted a seed that could grow into anything. No means freedom. Once someone has said no to you, you can relax and ask for even more. There is nothing for you, or the other person, to lose. There is no mutual commitment, so you can both explore all the options.

I am constantly presenting my value proposition to prospects. I get 10 times more nos than yesses—and I *expect* to

NO means
it's Never
Over until
you get to yes.

hear no because I'm the one who is proactively reaching out to others. I bring them possibilities that they didn't consider before. I make promises they haven't heard before. They were succeeding before I approached them. I represent change. I also represent risk.

In the beginning of every conversation, I haven't earned others' trust, especially when the stakes are high. If I get an easy or immediate yes, I regard it as a bonus. I see it as a gift that energizes me to go for even more nos. *No* is a person's default position. It's a defence as well as a way of buying time to consider your value proposition without the pressure to say yes. It's also an invitation to raise your game and enhance your offer.

Remember, every time you introduce something new, someone is going to say no. But many nos make a yes. NO means it's Never Over until you get to yes. There are always more ideas in your mental reservoir. There is always spare capacity that you haven't yet used. You can always take one extra step. That's why, as Billy Joel sings, sometimes you need to go to extremes: "Too high or too low—there ain't no in-betweens."

See the extra step as insurance-in-action: if you lose, you will always regret not taking it. But even if you lose, you'll never regret taking it. If you win because you take it, you'll always celebrate taking it.

Nos are packed with clues on how to get to yes. They are the staple diet of champions. Just like you need your daily requirement of vitamins and minerals, you need your daily nos.

MAKE YOUR BREAKTHROUGH

Go for No

Identify five HVPs: Highly Valuable Persons. These are key prospects who will benefit from your unique value proposition and help you achieve your prize. They could be people to whom you haven't presented before. Or they could be people who said no to you in the past. Either way, they represent pure upside that isn't currently being tapped.

1 Package your value proposition in a way that will capture their imagination, but present the opportunity to them in a way that doesn't push for the immediate "yes." Let them know you understand that they cannot commit immediately. Dial up your level of daring. Feel the fear and make it work for you. Make a powerful promise that will take everything you have to deliver. Earn the right to return with an even better offer. You have nothing to lose except your inertia.

2 Follow through on your commitment to follow through. Ask your peers how you can make a deeper impact. Collaborate with other stakeholders to expand your value proposition. Have some fun. Make some noise. Ask questions like:

   a Have you ever considered...?
   b What would happen if...?
   c How would you feel if...?

> **d** What would make the decisive difference?
>
> **e** What does the customer really want that they're not getting from anyone else?
>
> **3** Keep your pipeline full of HVPs. At any moment, ensure that you have 20 to 30 HVPs that you can call. Then call at least two of them every day. Make these calls a core discipline. Somebody, somewhere is just waiting to accept your offer.
>
> **4** Celebrate the conversation. Give up your dependence on "yes." Do it for the love of excellence and contribution. Enjoy the experience just for the sake of it. Success will eventually follow.

Love Your Competition

I often hear clients state that they hate their competition. They talk about wanting to kill or obliterate them. The truth is that they are only as good as their competition makes them. The quality of our rivals determines the quality of our performance. As tennis star Roger Federer said, "You cannot be alone at the top. You need rivals." Complacency is a temptation to which we will all succumb without others to stretch and test us. It's hard to keep the pedal to the metal.

Even when we're competing with each other, we're really collaborating in pursuit of superior performance. There are no winners without a contest. Too many wins lead to hubris. Too many losses means you're being left behind. The right balance breeds humility and learning in equal measure.

The 2018 World Series Champions, the Boston Red Sox, won 67 percent of their regular season games. The 2019 Stanley Cup Champions, the St. Louis Blues, won 55 percent of their regular season games. The 2020 NFL champions, the Tampa Bay Buccaneers, won 69 percent of their games. The 2021 NBA champions, the Milwaukee Bucks, won 64 percent of their games.

The best teams in the world lose at least 30 percent of the time. It keeps the taste of defeat in their mouths while they stay hungry for victory. Winning doesn't go to their heads and losing doesn't go to their hearts; they know they need both to be champions.

After they were beaten by the Toronto Raptors in the 2019 NBA finals, the Golden State Warriors ran a full-page advertisement in the *Toronto Star* congratulating their rivals. It showed their franchise player Steph Curry embracing Raptors point guard Kyle Lowry. The heading read, "The Golden State Warriors congratulate the Toronto Raptors on their historic achievement and bringing the 2019 NBA Championship to the city of Toronto." It was a classy appreciation of the role their rivals play in their sustained success as a team.

MAKE YOUR BREAKTHROUGH

Know Your Competitors

Right now, identify three competitors that are setting the pace in your space. Don't just think of the companies. Identify the actual people who exemplify excellence. Find out the actual steps they're taking to achieve success. Do your homework on their digital activities. Keep track of them in a document or spreadsheet. Talk to their customers or colleagues. Then decide how you can leapfrog them in a way that's right for your brand.

Consciously Create Your Best Reality through Homeostasis

If you drive a Mercedes-Benz, Audi or BMW, you know that all three brands recommend that you use only premium gasoline in your vehicle. High-performance machines need high-performance fuel. And it's the same for human beings. We cannot play like champions if we're running on rubbish. Junk foods lead to junk moods. We become what we eat. The data is decisive: diet is as important to our psychology as it is to our cardiology, endocrinology and gastroenterology.

But diet is just the beginning. Dr. Melissa Cugliari, a leading Toronto naturopathic doctor and lifestyle coach, believes that homeostasis is the key to sustained high performance. She says that "homeostasis is a self-regulating process by which we maintain internal equilibrium while adjusting to external conditions. It is dynamic and different for each person, depending on their mindset, physiology and life situations." Homeostasis provides you with the internal balance to handle external volatility. It's the sum total of what we think, do and eat.

Dr. Cugliari has identified 10 simple personal best practices that will empower us to consciously create our best reality if we turn them into non-negotiable daily habits. Check them out:

1 **Establish an optimal morning routine.** This includes maintaining a consistent wake time; consuming 500 mL to 1 L of room-temperature filtered water upon waking; practicing gratitude; and having breakfast within one hour of rising.

2 **Follow an essential exercise regimen.** This includes a 30-minute brisk walk or other cardiovascular exercise of your choosing; 30 minutes of resistance training and/or stretching daily; and setting a reminder on your phone, each hour, to get up and get some water, and stretch briefly before returning to work.

3 **Get grounded with meditation and breathwork.** Practice prana (breathwork). Take one-minute breaks every hour to deep breathe. This entails inhaling and exhaling deeply for three to four seconds each time. Focus on exhaling doubt and breathing in confidence each time.

4 **Develop a healthy hydration habit.** Your weight (in pounds) divided by two is the amount of water (in ounces) you need to drink *daily*. Workouts require an extra 500 mL. Herbal teas count. Frequency matters—so drink on the hour, every hour.

5 **Feast on superfoods.** Consume one cup of organic or wild-caught berries (fresh or frozen in smoothies) for longevity and vitality every day. To boost your brain function, eat wild-caught fish (wild salmon, anchovies, sardines) three to five times a week and drink two cups of organic

green tea (sencha, jasmine or other unflavoured varieties) daily. And to strengthen immune support, consume orange vegetables (carrots, sweet potatoes) and vitamin C-rich fruits (sliced organic lemon in water, an orange or an organic apple) daily.

6 **Seek out smart supplements.** Have your blood tested for vitamin D seasonally in late fall or early winter. Begin supplementation of 1,000 IU of vitamin D in September. Also take targeted multivitamins, based on your sex, age and nutritional needs. Seek advice from a professional about which supplements are best for you.

7 **Take care of your gut—build fibre into your daily diet.** Gut feel is real. A healthy gut communicates with the brain through nerves and hormones, which helps maintain general health and wellbeing. High levels of dietary fibre help maintain bowel health, lower blood cholesterol and sugar levels and aid in achieving healthy weight. You can build these daily sources of fibre into your diet: 2 tablespoons of ground flax, chia seeds, and/or psyllium husk (or a combination); 1 cup whole organic grains (rice, quinoa, steel-cut oats); ½ cup legumes (lentils, chickpeas, beans); 8 servings of vegetables (approximately 4–6 cups total); 2 servings of fruit (approximately 1 cup).

8 **Practice the art of effective eating.** Be mindful of the food you're eating. Relish every mouthful. Chew thoroughly. Eat away from your workspace. Have dinner two to three hours before bedtime. And stop when you are 80 percent full.

9 Embrace the social dividend. Connect with family members or other loved ones at least once each day via phone or text if you're not physically with them. Romantically connect with your partner daily. Reach out to your friends. Tell people how much you appreciate them. Keep making deposits into your social capital account, online or in person.

10 Wind down at night. Keep cell phones and screens out of the bedroom. Charge your phone in your bathroom or away from the bedroom in order to promote restful sleep. Start to dim lights half an hour before bedtime. Read a hardcopy book or magazine. Brew yourself a cup of lavender tea. Take a bath. Meditate, pray or engage in gratitude practice. Never go to sleep angry. Let go of whatever happened during the day. Look forward to dreamland.

Robust resilience is as much physical as it is mental. You can hide many things, but you cannot hide your lack of commitment to staying healthy. It's the first thing that people notice about you: either you look healthy or you don't. You look like you care about your body or you don't. You look like you have discipline or you don't. If you want to be the Potentiator, you need to model your own message. If you talk the talk, you must walk the walk.

If you feel like you've aged disproportionately during the pandemic, it's because you probably have. Chronic stress, the kind that is unrelenting, accelerates the rate of aging. Stress hampers the body's ability to repair itself—and the effects go beyond what you can see in the mirror. The good news is that you can slow—and even turn back—the clock by converting Dr. Cugliari's personal best practices into habits.

Either you control stress or the stress controls you. If you control the stress, it can become *eustress*: the kind of stress that is beneficial to your wellbeing. It sharpens you up, just as writing this book is sharpening me right now. It's the stress that I've chosen to experience. If the stress controls you, it turns into *distress*—the anxiety, pain or suffering that can wear you out from within.

Stick-With-It-Ness Is at the Heart of Robust Resilience

How strongly do you agree with the statement: "Once I start something, I stick with it until I am satisfied with the results"?

If you answered "strongly" or "totally," you're in the shrinking minority of Americans and Canadians. Environics research shows a consistent and significant decline in this trait over the past 30 years. It's down to about 35 percent of Americans and 30 percent of Canadians—a decline that betrays increasing distraction, decreasing patience and sheer fatigue.

We all know that nothing worthwhile comes easily or fast. But that doesn't register at a visceral level. It's hard to stick with it—especially when you run into roadblocks or fall down rabbit holes. That's when you need to remember why you signed up in the first place. If you can't recall a reason, you're going to give up way before the finish line. Then quitting becomes a habit, especially when you rationalize that you're not really quitting, it's just not worth the effort.

Tenacity in Canada and the U.S.

% who "strongly" (U.S.) or "totally" (Canada) agree that "Once I start
something, I stick with it until I am satisfied with the results."

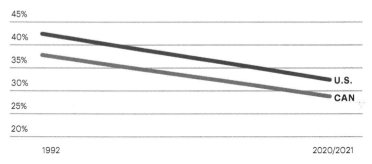

SOURCE: *Environics US Social Values Survey, 1992 and 2020; Environics Canadian
Social Values Survey, 1992 and 2021 (© 2021 Environics Research, all rights reserved)*

Let me ask you another question. How strongly do you
agree with the statement: "When I really want to do something, I almost always do it"?

If you answered "strongly" or "totally," you're in the top
quartile of all Americans or Canadians. You've got a built-in
motivator that makes you take action. You turn desire into
outcomes—you know that something always comes from
something but nothing comes from nothing.

So are you a doer? Or just a wisher? Have you become so
used to regret that it feels inevitable? Or are you activating
your dreams, one flawed step at a time? Hey, that's what I'm
doing right now. The fact that you're reading these words is
proof that it's worth it. Minimize your regret now. Procrasti-
nate later.

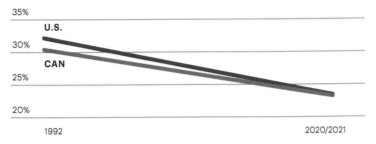

Commitment in Canada and the U.S.

% who "strongly" (U.S.) or "totally" (Canada) agree that
"When I really want to do something, I almost always do it."

SOURCE: *Environics US Social Values Survey, 1992 and 2020; Environics Canadian Social Values Survey, 1992 and 2021* (© *2021 Environics Research, all rights reserved*)

Practice for Real: Be Worthy of Your Gifts

No matter what your natural gifts, robust resilience requires a Herculean level of practice. Practice is defined as repeated performance or systematic exercise for the purposes of acquiring skill or proficiency. When you practice for real, you are always intentionally searching for ways to elevate your game. Every action is a gateway to greater impact.

Consider the winningest Olympian of all time, swimmer Michael Phelps. Phelps has won 28 medals—23 of them gold—in four Olympic games. He is six feet four inches tall. His wingspan is six feet seven inches. He has huge palms and wears a size 14 shoe. His torso is that of someone who is six feet eight inches tall, which is incredibly long. This empowers him with expanded reach to pull his way through the water. His body produces only half the lactic acid that his competitors need to manage.

In other words, Phelps is almost half amphibian. He is literally designed to be aquatic. The only thing missing is a set of gills. However, Phelps would not have become Phelps without training six hours a day, six days a week. In addition to swimming 80 kilometres a week, he also completed a rigorous weightlifting regimen three times a week. Overlaying all of this was his actual participation in multiple swim meets every season. Phelps's gifts were nothing without the willingness to develop them to the max.

Let's now go from winning Olympic gold to becoming a very different kind of gold standard. Shouldice Hospital is a facility located in Thornhill, about 20 kilometres north of downtown Toronto. It specializes in repairing abdominal wall hernias. Since its inception in 1945, it has made over 400,000 successful hernia repairs using a "natural tissue technique."

On its website, Shouldice claims that its surgical team is "comprised of the most experienced hernia surgeons in the world who have set the gold standard in hernia repair for decades by producing the lowest recorded rates for hernia recurrence and post-operative complications in the world." Shouldice encourages patients to "ensure your surgeon specializes in hernia repair, as there is no substitute for training and experience. All studies confirm that surgical outcomes improve with surgical repetition and volume."

The same truth applies to everything in life: the more we practice our craft, the better we become. But this is a different kind of practice. It is practice-for-real. Every time a Shouldice surgeon performs a hernia operation, they are acutely intentional in their actions. They are operating with deep expertise

Luck favours the brave— and the well prepared.

and they are enhancing their skill at the same time. They are refining their "natural tissue technique" with every surgery. Practice-for-real means preparing while you play. It's not a dry run or a dress rehearsal for the actual event. It *is* the actual event. There is no substitute for the pressure applied by the operating theatre or the boardroom or the basketball court or the baseball diamond. Winning is usually done by people who "have been there before." BGT—Big Game Temperament—is the hallmark of the great ones. They thrive on the intensity of big stakes. They don't obsess about the consequences of failure. They act in a way that enhances their effectiveness, over and over again.

The Potentiator is motivated by, not discouraged by, competition. Michael Phelps swam faster because he was racing against world-class rivals. The quality of his rivals determined the quality of his performance.

Relax, Get Ready, Get Going

We don't need to consult the Weather Network to know that storms are coming. Tsunamis begin long before they hit the shore. No matter what you do for a living, now would be a good time to prepare for the turbulence ahead.

Roald Amundsen led the first expedition to the South Pole in 1911. He also led the first expedition that was proved to have reached the North Pole in 1926, and died two years later while on a rescue mission in the Artic. Amundsen epitomized robust resilience when he said, "Victory awaits him who has everything in order—luck we call it. Defeat is definitely due for him who has neglected to take the necessary precautions—bad luck we call it."

Luck favours the brave—and the well prepared. You may not be able to anticipate every problem. But you can be actively ready to solve them as they arise. The question is not, "Why is this happening to me?" It is "Why *not* me?" and "How can I make this my finest moment?" Sometimes you can choose your situation. And sometimes you can choose only your attitude toward your situation. Either way, it's always your choice.

Not all times in life are created equal. Being the source of other people's hope in the face of panic will take all you have—and then some. You must know when you can indulge in your doubts and when to be resolute for others. You can go through doubt and ennui on a Sunday evening as long as you get into the game on Monday. In-between moments are when you relax and recharge for the moments that matter. Even the Potentiator needs time-outs. Burnout is not an option. Sometimes, you just need to take yourself out of the game.

Shutting down is as important as starting up. By definition, when you're the Potentiator you have a lot on your plate. You're up to big things. At any moment, you're pursuing a variety of ventures with a plethora of people. The chance of something going wrong on some of their projects is almost certain. Learning not to worry is as important as anything else.

I have a figurative off-switch in my brain that I flick at 9 p.m. most evenings; anything that hasn't been resolved by then can be resumed early the next morning. Nine at night until six in the morning is my "safe time." I've made it through another day. I've earned a couple hours of complete relaxation and a good night's sleep. When I awake the next morning, I'm ready to take on the new day: refreshed, recharged and robustly resilient.

3

The Third
Potentiator Practice
Grow
Courageous
Creativity

You can't use up creativity. The more you use the more you have.

MAYA ANGELOU

A FLOCK OF birds walk into a bar. They look around, then they head for the door. The bartender says, "Hey, what's the matter?" One of the birds says, "This place looked seedier from the outside."

An empty bottle walks into a bar. The bartender says, "I can't serve you. You're already drunk."

A five dollar bill walks into a bar. The bartender says, "Sorry, this is a singles bar."

I hope you're chuckling. I also hope that you find "walk into a bar" jokes as satisfying as I do. In the cold light of reason, they're ludicrous. In the foolish light of humour, they're bizarrely funny. Why? Because when it comes to jokes, we suspend our disbelief. The phrase, "Let me tell you a joke..." uncouples what we're about to hear from our day-to-day realities. In the world of "walk into a bar" jokes, of course a flock of birds, empty bottles and dollar bills can walk into a bar.

And of course a bartender would anthropomorphize them. After all, birds, bottles and dollar bills have feelings too, don't they? Anything is possible when you liberate yourself from the notions "That will never work" or "That doesn't make sense" or "That's impossible."

Creativity is the ability to see the world in new ways. It's finding hidden patterns that enable others to make sense of things that don't make sense. It's seeing the relationships between disassociated phenomena and communicating them to others. It's the ability to think of new ideas and make new things from them. It's plumbing the depths of our imagination to conjure up new possibilities. It's packaging existing concepts in a novel way that enables people to process them differently. It's finding fresh solutions to old problems and old solutions to fresh problems.

Most of all, creativity is freedom. Freedom from the pull of your past, from the fear of your future, from the concerns about looking stupid to others, from the need to fit in, from the constrictions of your personal identity, from the established rules of the game. Creativity is the elixir that enables you to transcend the gravity of "what is" in order to manifest "what can be."

What would you do if you weren't afraid to fail? What risks would you take? Who would you reach out to? What territories would you explore? What moonshot would you take? How would you express your inner genius?

Now ask yourself what you're forfeiting by not following all those avenues. Without being reckless or irresponsible, what could you pursue that would express your inner genius and potentiate the people around you? To quote the band Nickelback, "What are you, what are you waiting for?" It's unlikely that you'll find the perfect moment. But you can find one that's perfect enough, because that's entirely up to you. In fact, this may be it. It's time to get curious: the state of being eager to learn, investigate or know more.

In their 2020 book *The Curious Advantage*, Paul Ashcroft, Simon Brown, and Garrick Jones make the case that creativity—and specifically, the curious environment that gives birth to creativity—"is the greatest driver of value in the new digital age. Curiosity is at the heart of the skills required to successfully navigate our digital lives when all futures are uncertain."

How Creative Are You?

Ask yourself, "How creative am I?" Is your answer "not at all" or "so-so" or "not very"? If so, you are not alone.

Most people don't see themselves as creative and imaginative. They were either told, or told themselves (and, often, early on in life), that compared to others (or, worse, in absolute terms) they just weren't naturally artistic, or weren't good at solving problems, or weren't really ideas people. Perhaps they believe creativity is a rare commodity—one that is awarded sparingly to only a few gifted people.

These beliefs are both self-defeating and false. As humans, we have proven powers of almost infinite invention and imagination. Yet most of us don't credit ourselves with that capacity. According to Environics Social Values research, only 30 percent of Americans and 20 percent of Canadians are confident in their creative ability and power of imagination.

Just think about what that means: if you don't even see *yourself* as creative or imaginative, you are not likely to manifest those traits. You are going to give up your power to the small minority who believe in their creative superpower. On the other hand, if you are the small minority, you have an embedded competitive advantage over 70 percent of the population!

Self-Identification as Personally Creative

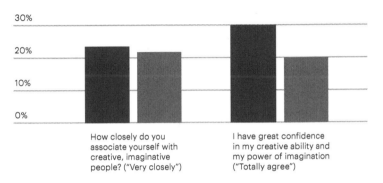

SOURCE: *Environics US Social Values Survey, 2020; Environics Canadian Social Values Survey, 2021 (© 2021 Environics Research, all rights reserved)*

According to David Brodzinsky, a professor of developmental and clinical psychology at Rutgers University, "Our identity is what grounds us and gives our lives meaning. This identity can be a motivating force or a debilitating one depending on how we define ourselves and internalize the feedback we get from others." If you don't perceive yourself as creative or imaginative, you cripple that capacity at its source.

Courageous creativity may require an intense course in intentional unlearning so you can reverse a lifetime of misinterpretation or underestimation of your talents. What do you need to unlearn? What misguided injunctions have dominated your life? Personally, I was taught that the pursuit of wealth was wrong. I was raised with the belief that other people didn't really care about me. I was told that small talk was a waste of time. I was warned against embracing popular culture. I'm still seeking to disabuse myself of these notions—but at least I'm aware of them.

Most of us need the Potentiator in our lives to banish these myths and help liberate our creativity. They are the ones who help us see what we *can* be—regardless of what we believe ourselves to *have* been. When you become the Potentiator, this may be the most important breakthrough you create with others. I acknowledge all the Potentiators who enabled me to come this far. Take a moment to think about *your* Potentiators—then reach out to them and acknowledge their contribution to your evolution. There is no greater compliment you can pay them.

Creativity Thrives in a Beginner's Mind

It's no coincidence that creativity is most often associated with youth. Beginners have a poorly developed sense of the odds against them. They are untrammelled by tradition and unburdened by legacy. They are not protecting the status quo that they helped build. They don't know that it can't be done—so they go ahead and do it. They are idealistic about the future. They believe in their ability to make an impact. Their enthusiasm is powerful mojo.

Gen Z (those born after 1995) and Millennials (born between 1980 and 1995) are acknowledged by many as the most creative generations. Technology has enabled them to see, do and connect with things that were inaccessible to

previous generations. There is a reason why they are not prepared to "pay their dues," like older generations expect. They
believe they have a better way and are determined to prove
it. Their mantra is "challenge convention." Perhaps no Millennial better personifies this trend, this mantra, than Mark
Zuckerberg (b. 1984), whose Facebook empire challenged
convention and changed the way we communicate forever.

Millennials also feel the stress of the moment more than
other generations. According to a 2020 Deloitte Global Millennial Survey, close to half (48 percent) of Gen Z and 44
percent of Millennial respondents said they're stressed all or
most of the time. But they are also an idealistic generation:
nearly three-fourths said the pandemic has made them more
sympathetic toward others' needs and that they intend to take
actions to have a positive impact on their communities. Also,
contrary to the stereotype, they're quite loyal: more Millennials said they'd like to stay with their employers for at least five
years than would prefer to leave within two years. According
to Deloitte, this is unprecedented since the consultancy first
asked this question in its 2016 survey.

If Millennials are worried about being future-ready, what
should older generations be thinking? The good news is that a
recent study conducted by the US Census Bureau and two MIT
professors found that the most successful entrepreneurs tend
to be middle-aged—even in the tech sector. The researchers
compiled a list of 2.7 million company founders who hired at
least one employee between 2007 and 2014. The average
startup founder was 45 years old when they founded one of
the most successful tech companies. And in general terms,
a 50-year-old entrepreneur is almost two times more likely

There is no substitute for repeated confrontations with crucible challenges.

to start an extremely successful company than a 30-year-old and almost three times more likely than a 25-year-old.

And if you want a really fun statistic: a 60-year-old startup founder is three times more likely to found a successful startup than a 30-year-old startup founder. How is that possible? Age and experience can be powerful multipliers of youth and enthusiasm. Wisdom is hard won.

Longevity is its own competitive advantage. There is no substitute for repeated confrontations with crucible challenges. These are the moments of severe trial in which several elements interact, leading to the creation of something new. Each one is an infusion into the creativity reservoir.

Unleash Your Imagination: Be a Perennial

Being a Millennial is a function of birth date; being a Perennial is a function of mindset. Unlike annual or biennial plants that die after one to two seasons, a perennial is a plant (like a rose or a geranium) that flowers year after year. A Perennial person is someone who does likewise. They are always new because they're always reinventing themselves in sync with their environments. Age is just a number if your spirit is forever young.

Glenda Jackson, the legendary two-time Oscar-winning actor, is a Perennial. In the spring of 2019, at the age of 82—after two decades as a member of the UK parliament—she returned to acting in the role of King Lear. King Lear is regarded by many as the toughest male role in all of Shakespeare's plays. Being an octogenarian woman made it even tougher. In an interview with the *New York Times Magazine*,

Jackson described the extent of her nightly performance: "In a strange kind of way, you should have nothing to take home. You should have put everything that has to be put on that stage. Shame on you if you have something to take home."

Compared to Jackson, how much of yourself are you investing in your day-to-day activities? How much more could you do if you were curious and committed enough to find out how far you could go? What could you achieve if you were willing to unleash your imagination and follow it wherever it chooses to go? How much is riding on your discovery of a better way? Who is depending on you to help them get ahead? How much does it even matter to you?

Clint Eastwood is another Perennial. At the age of 88, he produced, directed and starred in the 2018 blockbuster movie *The Mule*. Eastwood plays the role of an octogenarian drug runner for a Mexican cartel into the US. The movie's budget was $50 million; it grossed over $170 million. In a conversation with Toby Keith, the country singer, Eastwood shared his personal mantra: "I never let the old man in." This inspired Keith to write the title song for the film, "Don't Let the Old Man In."

The great baseball player Satchel Paige once asked, "How old would you be if you didn't know how old you are?" What would your answer be? And why? I would be 35. That's the age I was when I delivered my first professional keynote. It was a thrilling renaissance out of a time of personal darkness and doubt. I still experience the same sense of magic every time I get up to speak.

As a self-declared Potentiator, I am heartened and disheartened by the latent power that people are carrying around within them. I'm heartened by the potential of people to produce remarkable results, but I'm disheartened by the disinclination of many people to turn their latent power into real power. *Latent* is defined as existing but not yet fully developed—dormant or hidden until circumstances are suitable for manifestation. Latent talent needs to be intentionally activated.

Some kind of wake-up call is required for people to unleash their imagination. In the cases of Jackson and Eastwood, it's a natural drive fused with extraordinary talent. In my case, it was a prolonged struggle with clinical depression in my early 30s that prompted me to become a motivational speaker—partially as a way of vaccinating myself against the disease. Now, in my early 60s, it's the hunger for relevance and appetite for adventure. To quote the great Springsteen, "Now some guys they just give up living / And start dying little by little, piece by piece / Some guys come home from work and wash up / And go racin' in the street."

What is it for you?

Questions Are the Answer

Even though this book is a one-way communication, from me to you, I am continually aiming to spark your thinking by asking you the best questions that I can. I'm counting on you to do the deep work—grapple with the concepts, dialogue with your associates, and push the envelope even further. Here are some of my favourite phrases to kick-start your imagination:

* I wonder whether...?
* How about...?
* What would happen if...?

* Why is ... happening?
* Why is ... not happening?
* Do you think ...?
* Could we try ...?
* Who could help us?
* Where should we be looking?
* Why is now the right time to act?

In my coaching sessions with C-suite clients, I encourage them to come to each session with consequential questions that could lead to innovative ideas and actions. Otherwise, they just come prepared to answer my questions—because that's what they are trained to do. They believe they are expected to know the answers, whereas the best leaders are really expected to know the *questions*.

In an October 2006 interview with *Time* magazine, Eric Schmidt, the former CEO of Google and a leading business thinker, said, "We run the company by questions, not by answers ... Out of the conversation comes innovation. Innovation is not something [where] I just wake up one day and say, 'I want to innovate.' I think you get a better innovative culture if you ask it as a question."

MAKE YOUR BREAKTHROUGH

The Imagination Checkpoints

How do you even know if you have unleashed your imagination? Here are Lipkin's five checkpoints. On each checkpoint, rate yourself 2 for yes, 1 for sometimes, 0 for no.

1 You are feeling challenged, excited and fulfilled by your work.

Yes   Sometimes   No

2 You are surprising yourself with the calibre of your ideas and actions.

Yes   Sometimes   No

3 You are generating new ideas and trying new approaches.

Yes   Sometimes   No

4 You are perceived as the best in the game.

Yes   Sometimes   No

5 You are receiving feedback from colleagues and customers that you are stimulating their ideation and inspiring them into effective action.

Yes   Sometimes   No

If you scored 8 out of 10 or higher, you've unleashed your imagination. Now you need to keep feeding your fire. If you scored above 5 out of 10, you're in the right arena. Now you need to sharpen your sword. If you scored under 5, treat this as your wake-up call. Your competitor may also be reading these words right now.

David versus Goliath: Courageous Creativity Is Literally a Giant-Slayer

In the biblical tale of David versus Goliath, David is a shepherd boy who volunteers to take on the enemy giant, Goliath, because everyone else in his tribe is afraid to. As it is written in 1 Samuel 17 (NIV), they were "dismayed and terrified" and "they all fled from him in great fear."

David's fellow tribesmen saw a nine-foot-nine warrior clad head-to-toe in bronze armor. They visualized their death at his hands. They compared their puny status to his oversized presence. David, on the other hand, saw someone who was less dangerous than the lions and bears he slew as part of his everyday job. He was buoyed by the courage that he had earned protecting his flock. He was far more excited than he was afraid.

David also saw three things that no one else saw. One, Goliath was hampered, not strengthened, by his armor. Two, he was fighting with a sword, spear and javelin—weapons that limited his range and mobility. Three, he didn't know what to make of David. Goliath was half insulted, half confused by David's youth and non-combatant clothing.

As the story is told, David refused to don the armor that was offered to him. His vision did not include getting up close and personal with Goliath. He was empowered by an entirely different paradigm. So he chose five smooth stones from a nearby stream, put them in the pouch of his shepherd's bag and, with his sling in his hand, he approached Goliath. As the giant moved toward him, David ran quickly toward the battle line to meet him. He used his speed and nimbleness to outmaneuver Goliath, place a stone in his sling and hurl it at him. It hit Goliath with force in the centre of his forehead, killing him instantly.

David was fighting a different fight from Goliath, with a different weapon. Goliath was looking for a close-range encounter where he could stab David to death. David leveraged his sling technology to kill Goliath remotely. In hindsight, Goliath didn't stand a chance. It wasn't just David's superior equipment; it was his certainty in the outcome. While Goliath was hobbled by complacency and outraged by the affront to his ego, David was single-minded in his mission to slay his nemesis.

David was also motivated by money. The first question that he asked when he considered fighting Goliath was, "What will be done for the man who kills this Philistine?" The answer was great wealth, the king's daughter and a lifetime tax exemption. David wasn't a zealot. He was a mercenary. He seized the moment to catapult himself into instant fame, fortune and power.

My question to you is: What battle are you fighting? What approach are you using? Are you enslaved by conventional wisdom and status quo? Or are you rewriting the rules of engagement? Just like David, you have frequent opportunities to slay your personal Goliaths. You just may not have thought of them like that. Now would be a good time to look at your biggest challenges through a fresh set of lenses.

Imagineering in the Age of "the Constant Pivot"

We are living in the age of "the constant pivot." Every day requires either minor or wholesale adjustments to both strategy and execution. It could be a regulatory change, a competitive move, a global trade war, a customer shift, a new government, a technological innovation, a product recall, an interest rate increase or a Covid variant. No matter what your role, you are going to have to unleash your imagination—your creativity—to play it well.

Knowledge is key—but imagination is even more important, because imagination is what you do with knowledge. Knowledge is about the past and present. Imagination is about the future.

Imagineer is a term trademarked by Disney. It comes from the fusion of *imagine* and *engineer*, and it expresses the ability to turn ideas into reality, whether it is a new attraction at Disney World or just a way to enable your team to play better. Small successes line the road to big wins. So what questions will you ask today to *imagineer* your future? Where will you go today? What will you do today? If you want to unearth diamonds, find out where they are. Then get to work—just like Seth Meyers, Alice Chang and Neil Dipaola.

Seth Meyers, host of NBC's *Late Night with Seth Meyers*, is an imagineer who resonates deeply with me. Four nights a week, Meyers tapes his show at 6:30 p.m. for broadcast at 12:35 a.m. Meyers encapsulates the news of the day and all its weirdness with "emergency room urgency," according to *Fast Company* magazine. Meyers and his team test the nightly material with live audiences at 4 p.m., ahead of the taping. This enables

If you want to unearth diamonds, find out where they are.

———

them to present a fine-tuned package of clarity and humour as part of the show. As Meyers says, "I think that the best thing we can hope to provide is the catharsis of laughter with a subject that people wouldn't otherwise be laughing at." Meyers lives the mantra of "Many a true word is said in jest."

Alice Chang is an example of an imagineer who was ahead of her time. Chang founded her Taiwanese tech company, Perfect Corp., in 2014—and over the past few years has introduced a variety of AI and AR tools for the beauty industry. During the pandemic, however, her business was transformed—retailers shut down, and in-store sampling of makeup and lipstick became impossible. During 2020, Perfect reported a 32 percent increase in consumer use of virtual try-on tools by major brands—and in December 2020, the company partnered with Snapchat to bring AR try-on experiences into its social media platform. Chang is an example of an imagineer who is not only solving a problem of today, but also opening up a world of opportunity for tomorrow—introducing beauty brands—to new generations of customers.

"Even before the pandemic, people were growing apprehensive to [sic] community testers and [had] hygiene worries," said Chang. "With the rise of global health concerns surrounding the pandemic, physical testers are quickly being replaced by hyper-realistic digital try-on experiences." Perfect Corp.'s business model includes both B2B and B2C components, with over 300 B2B brand partners, such as Estée Lauder and NARS, and 900 million global downloads of its own app.

Neil Dipaola is the co-founder and CEO of AutoCamp. Their mission is to reimagine the way you experience the outdoors. They epitomize the "glamping" trend by revolutionizing both camping and luxury accommodation. They promise "Adventure Simplified," hosting guests in chic Airstream travel trailers or luxury tents in Russian River, Yosemite and Santa Barbara, California. They are also exploring other sites across the US. Dipaola says it costs 30 to 40 percent less to construct an AutoCamp than a traditional hotel. The rooms are also easy to set up and move.

AutoCamp is clearly an idea whose time is come, especially post-pandemic. But it took a hospitality evangelist like Dipaola to turn it into reality. He has also raised $115 million to secure land and install facilities in other iconic locations like Cape Cod, Massachusetts. If you can imagineer it, they will come.

Experiment like Edison, Bezos or Dyson

Thomas Edison is one of the most celebrated inventors in American history. His tenacious commitment to innovation was evidenced by his development of 10,000 prototypes of the lightbulb before he created a commercially viable version. As he is quoted as saying, "I have not failed 10,000 times. I have not failed once. I have succeeded in proving that those 10,000 ways will not work. When I have eliminated the ways that will not work, I will find the way that will work."

Edison's work around the lightbulb also enabled him to invent a range of other noteworthy products, including the alkaline battery, an electric generator, the phonograph, the automatic telegraph and an ore separator that extracted magnetic substances from non-magnetic. These inventions were partially a result of his pursuit of the lightbulb. Unsuccessful attempts to invent the lightbulb were repurposed into other inventions. His constant experimentation was the genesis of his genius ideas. Even when he didn't get the results he expected, he was generating results that produced the unexpected.

The 21st-century commercial heir to Edison is Jeff Bezos, founder and CEO of Amazon. In his letter to shareholders on April 5, 2016, he wrote:

> To invent you have to experiment, and if you know in advance that it's going to work, it's not an experiment. Outsized returns often come from betting against conventional wisdom, and conventional wisdom is usually right. We all know that if you swing for the fences, you're going to strike out a lot, but you're also going to hit some home runs. The difference between baseball and business, however, is that baseball has a truncated outcome distribution. When you swing, no matter how well you connect with the ball, the most runs you can get is four. In business, every once in a while, when you step up to the plate, you can score 1,000 runs. This long-tailed distribution of returns is why it's important to be bold. Big winners pay for so many experiments.

James Dyson is another modern-day Edison epitomizing the ethos of experimentation. Dyson is the septuagenarian billionaire founder and chairman of his eponymous company. In 2021, it was announced that Dyson would invest £2.75 billion (about US$4 billion) over the next five years in robotics, artificial intelligence and other technologies as the company explores new markets and product areas. But it all began with a simple household product—the vacuum cleaner—and Dyson's frustration with his family's appliance. In 1978, he set out to invent a better vacuum cleaner using a cyclone to lift dirt.

In a special for the *Globe and Mail* on August 11, 2014, Dyson wrote, "It took me 15 years and 5,127 attempts to develop the first bagless cyclonic vacuum... What matters about failure is that you learn from it... Creativity doesn't come from instructions, but the guts to look at something in a different way and question it." He also likes to draw on the freshness of youth: "If you visit any of our offices... you'll notice young people buzzing around everywhere. We hire inexperienced people, often straight out of university. Why? Because untried minds bring energy and expertise in places where, let's be frank, someone with my number of miles on the clock might not have."

As the Potentiator, you need to lead by example by swinging for the fences. Creating breakthroughs for others by helping them play at their best is a privilege that must be earned with a few home runs and many strikeouts. Before anyone is prepared to listen to you, they need to know your credentials as an experimenter, innovator and inventor. I've quoted Edison, Bezos and Dyson as archetypes of the species—and while I cannot lay claim to that level of greatness, I have, in my own way, swung for the fences as hard as I could.

I have authored eight books on personal development (including this one) and delivered over two thousand seminars around the world. This book is a culmination of my experience and my expertise. It has taken me almost three years to write. It was punctuated with false starts and frustrated hiatuses—and put on pause during the pandemic. It took me over a year just to get rid of the kitchen sink and find my focus. I experimented with different topics and titles. Eventually, I arrived at *The Potentiator* because I truly believe that the only way to get ahead is to help others get ahead. As I've established, to *potentiate* means to nudge people into actions that will benefit them while benefitting us. At the same time, we need to ensure that people attribute their success partially to the guidance that we have provided them. We need to become indispensable to their wellbeing. It's a form of benign Machiavellianism. So I enable people to achieve the outcomes that matter most to them while expanding their capacity to sustain remarkable performance—with my help, of course.

As I've inched forward in this process, I've created opportunities to test this hypotheses. I've aired the Potentiator Practices in seminars and workshops with clients and colleagues that wanted to participate in my content development. Like a pilot in a simulator, I've rehearsed these stories in friendly environments. That's how experimentation can actually be a safe activity.

Toastmasters epitomizes this notion. It is a global non-profit organization that teaches public speaking and leadership skills through an international network of clubs. It has 15,800-plus clubs across 149 countries. Most clubs have no more than 20 members. They follow a template set out by the Toastmasters headquarters.

Members sign up for a low monthly fee and meet once a week. They make presentations to their peers and receive constructive feedback. During the pandemic, many clubs went online—and set up tips and videos for club members on how to interact in a virtual world. But whether in "real life" or online, the animating focus remains the same: work collaboratively to improve each other's performance.

Each participant is a Potentiator. The brilliance of the concept is how it enables people to engage in a scary activity with zero risk. I began my speaking career by attending Toastmasters in Johannesburg, South Africa. And I will always be grateful for its foundational instruction. I have also endeavoured to replicate its lesson in my own programs. Whatever you say in my sessions, I am going to make you look good.

In the end, it may all come down to that: the need to look good or the fear of looking bad. The impostor syndrome is the bogeyman that bedevils our quest to become a better version of ourselves. We are afraid that we're not as good as other people think we are and, by experimenting and failing, we'll reveal our inferior selves to the world. As the cartoonist Walt Kelly wrote in his *Pogo* comic strip, "We have met the enemy and he is us."

Of course, there is the ever-present potential for damage, disaster and self-destruction. But thinking too vividly about it can become paralyzing. At any moment, our carefully constructed edifices can shatter and crumble. Every day, we experience near misses or close calls. One step farther or one second later may have ended in tears or even worse. It's best not to dwell on these almost-catastrophes because the opposite is also true. We often ascribe our wins to our skill and diligence, but the truth is that we are the beneficiaries of fortunate flukes in our favour more often than we recognize. Think about it the next time either outcome is experienced.

The vast majority of people do not have real enemies. They have competitors. They have rivals. They have acquaintances who may not like them or detractors who may not endorse them. But they don't have other people who purposely want to do them harm. However, in the absence of real enemies, people create them. Then they conjure up phantom fears. Courage may be simple common sense: other people don't care enough to hurt you. They have their own issues to handle. That's why they need your help.

Creativity Is Physical: Neurons That Fire Together, Wire Together

Just as our daily activity literally shapes our bodies, our daily thoughts literally shape our brains. Our experiences are restructuring our minds as we learn and adapt to new challenges. This is called neuroplasticity—the "muscle-building" part of the brain. Just as your pectoral, biceps or abdominal muscles respond to working out in a gym, your brain responds to conditioning.

With every repetition of a thought or emotion, we reinforce a neural pathway—the way our brain processes those thoughts or emotions. With each new repetition, we create a new way of interacting with the world. These shifts, repeated often enough, can change the way our brains work—for better or for worse.

First we make our habits. Then our habits make us. We become what we repeatedly do. If we are disciplined or inspired enough, we're willing to do the hard things that develop our capacity. If we're lax or lazy, we follow the path of least resistance. The choices are simple, but they're not easy. Accumulate flab or build muscle. Use it or lose it. Grow creativity or become irrelevant. It's that stark.

The danger of depression or indifference is that it impedes constructive action. It literally shrinks your neural network. Without the passion or optimism to power your motivation in the face of obstacles, courageous creativity will elude you. It's chemical. Positive emotions create the endorphins, oxytocin and dopamine, that enable extraordinary effort. If you don't find a way, you fade away. As Bruce Springsteen reminds us, we're all just "dancing in the dark." It's the willingness to search for the light that sparks the fire within.

Neuroplasticity never ends. Connections within the brain are constantly becoming stronger or weaker, depending on what is being used. When we're young, our bodies and brains change easily. As we age, we need to work harder at effecting change. We need greater patience and commitment to our internal evolution. We need to override the natural aging tendency toward rigidity and fixedness.

Right now, the good news is that you're building mental muscle. You're doing the right work. You're reinforcing the right neural networks. You're downloading the right content. You're learning a new kind of language. But this is just the beginning. How can you boldly go where you've never been before? What can you invent that encourages others to expand? What have you been postponing that you need to confront? Now is always a great time to act. You can be either a procrastinator or a Potentiator. They are mutually exclusive.

Things are unlikely to become more stable any time soon, so make unpredictability work for you. Embrace surprises while you surprise others. That's one of the reasons I wrote *The Potentiator*. I want to be more creative tomorrow than I was yesterday—by exploring a whole new realm of neural possibilities.

As a world authority on brain plasticity, Dr. Michael Merzenich writes in his book *Soft-Wired*, "If you're still alive at the age of 50 and you live in the United States or Europe, the average lifespan extends into the ninth decade of life. Just about every person who is reading this book can optimistically look forward to living past their 85th birthday. You should know, then, that at that age there is roughly a 50 percent chance that you will be formally identified as senile and demented."

How's that for a wake-up call? Growing courageous creativity, along with all the other Potentiator Practices, is a powerful protection against dementia. The best defence is a great offence. By training yourself to help others play at their best, you prolong your performance at your best.

MAKE YOUR BREAKTHROUGH

BYOE—Be Your Own Experiment

In the next month, identify one new approach, engage in one new venture or implement one new idea that enables you to boldly go where you've never gone before. It could be professional, personal or both. It must be big enough to expand your range and scare you just a little bit. Then identify another experiment— and another—until it becomes a way of being.

Courageous Creativity Takes Blood, Sweat and Tears—Let Them See What It Takes

Conventional macho wisdom declares that you should never let them see you sweat. My guidance is just the opposite: let them see how much of yourself you're investing in the moment. Exhibit your commitment to their success. Unveil your humanity. Make your effort transparent. Don't let others think that you're cruising in their presence. Slick and smooth has no traction with their hearts.

Your degree of visible effort is directly proportional to the respect you have for your stakeholders. If you're just mailing it in, you're signalling your lack of appreciation for others. You're putting your own comfort ahead of their return on time with you. No one is inspired by an automatic pilot.

In my keynotes and workshops, I share emotions that are bubbling just below the surface. I communicate how hard I have to work to make it look easy. I ensure that no one thinks that I'm taking them or the opportunity for granted.

I want people to see the real person behind the persona. I've discovered that trust is a function of people's belief in my authenticity. It takes courage to be vulnerable, but that's what it takes to have a heart-to-heart with whomever you're with. Anything less just won't cut it.

Talk, Listen and Learn

You can't grow courageous creativity by yourself. Problems happen in the real world and that's where they need to be

A simple sentence can become a life sentence for the people you're speaking to.

solved. Your guru is not sitting at the top of the mountain in splendid isolation. They are on the street or at a desk near you. When the student is ready, the teacher appears. If you're ready, everyone is your teacher. Your mind is like a parachute: it works better when it's open.

There is a well-worn saying that we have two ears and one mouth so we can listen twice as much as we speak. That may be so. But we should seize every opportunity to express our point of view because until we can convey our ideas to others, we don't know what we know. When we talk to ourselves, we're incredibly articulate. We're all opinion leaders in our own minds.

But there is a chasm of difference between the inside of our minds and the words coming out of our mouths. The first time we attempt to convert our thoughts into language, it can sound clumsy and clunky. Our speech is punctuated with "you knows" and "umms" and "kind ofs" and "seems likes." It's only after we've test-driven the statements a number of times with others that we can distill them into cogent concepts.

Stephen R. Covey, author of *The Seven Habits of Highly Effective People*, writes that the fifth habit is to "seek first to understand, then to be understood." If you're interested in others, you'll be interesting to others. However, you need to talk first. You need to reach out to them. You need to go where they are. Whatever your personal style, it's up to you to initiate the conversation.

The easier you make it for other people to talk to you, the more conversations you'll have with them. If you're not taking the time to talk to others, you're squandering an opportunity for potential pollination. You never know when you'll be able to germinate the insights you receive from others. But you do know that if you don't have the conversations in the first place, there is no chance of anything flowering later on.

As I have discovered, when you're the Potentiator, you invite others into your space. You ask the right questions. You verbalize the right responses. You earn the right to others' time and ideas.

Here are some Potentiator phrases that are guaranteed to encourage others to share their thoughts with you:

* I'm curious to understand how you do that.

* That's fascinating. Tell me more.

* That's amazing. I've never thought of it that way before.

* Wow! That's extraordinary. Can you help me understand what that takes?

* This makes perfect sense. What led you to this point?

* This is beautiful. What or who inspired you to create it?

* I'm impressed. What advice can you give me to achieve something similar?

* If you were starting from scratch like I am, what would your first steps be?

* I hear what you're saying, but can we go a little deeper? I want to know what's really behind your success.

In this book, learning isn't a sedentary activity—the simple acquisition of passive knowledge. It's a dance with partners that both lead and follow. Epiphanies are the results of joyful sweat. Even if you're talking to a stranger, you have to be willing to push the envelope. As long as you demonstrate an authentic curiosity and admiration for them, they will reveal their secrets to you. It's often easier to talk honestly with someone you don't know. There's no static interfering with the exchange.

The best compliments you can receive are when others say to you:

* I've never told anyone this before.

* I don't know why I'm saying this.

* Keep this confidential, but...

* You make it easy for me to express my point of view.

* No one has asked me those questions before.

* I like talking to you.

* Now that I hear myself say that, it makes even more sense to me.

* You say things in a way that helps me understand myself better.

As the Potentiator, you play your part in your social symbiosis with others. You feed the souls that feed you.

A simple sentence can become a life sentence for the people you're speaking to. So choose your language carefully. I'm continually astonished by the enduring impact of a wayward conversation on people's psyches. When I probe for why people act or think in a certain way, they often tell me about the advice they received from a boss, family member or trusted advisor. It embedded itself in their subconscious, automatically influencing their behaviour. Everyone is a composite of all the conversations that they have ever had. Be aware of your unconscious triggers and beware of seeding other minds with negative drivers.

MAKE YOUR BREAKTHROUGH

Practice Talking, Listening and Learning as if Every Conversation Is a Potential Breakthrough

In your next conversation, talk, listen and learn as though you're about to produce the outcome that matters most to everyone. Be cognizant of your energy, openness and engagement. Prepare questions that are likely to lead to the greatest breakthroughs. Make it safe for others to share their points of view by giving encouraging responses. Then keep doing it... in every conversation you have.

4

The Fourth
Potentiator Practice
Communicate Like a Champion

Words cut down trees. The axe is just an instrument.

AFRICAN PROVERB

D R. BETH ABRAMSON—director of the Cardiac Prevention and Rehabilitation Centre and Women's Cardiovascular Health at St. Michael's Hospital in Toronto—is one of the leading authorities on heart health in Canada. I was introduced to her when I was prescribed a revolutionary new medicine called Repatha to control my blood cholesterol. As a professional speaker, I was immediately struck by her communication skills. She epitomizes everything that will be discussed in this chapter.

You may not know Dr. Abramson, but you know someone like her: a medical, legal or financial professional who has saved your life, either literally or figuratively. These individuals share four extraordinary traits, best understood by the acronym CARE:

Clear: They are immediately understandable. They choose their words carefully. They speak deliberately. They make sure you can follow exactly what they're saying by asking, "Is that clear?" "Do you understand?" "Does that make sense to you?" "Do you have any questions?"

Authoritative: They are in total command of their subject matter. They talk with conviction and certainty. They have a specific point of view and are not ambivalent about their advice or recommended course of action.

Reassuring: They make you feel safe. They provide you with a sense of security that everything possible is being done on your behalf. They give you the perspective to see things in a positive light. They make you feel like someone strong is fighting a battle on your behalf, and you can rest easier knowing it.

Empowering: They tell you what they're going to do, and they instruct you on what you need to do, as a result of your conversations with them. They also alert you to the dangers or pitfalls that may await you, expanding your capacity to deal with challenges for which you are not trained.

In some shape, manner or form, we all need to demonstrate CARE in the way we communicate with our stakeholders. We may have different styles, personalities or philosophies, but the net result must be the same: people who are better off because we've communicated with them.

The quality of our communication determines the quality of our life. Language, both verbal and non-verbal, is like oxygen: very little happens without it. When communication is clean, clear and pure, we all breathe easier. We inhale inspiration and learning. Even the word "spirit" comes from the Latin word *spiritus*, which means breath. Great conversations open us up; they invigorate us. Grudge conversations do the opposite: they smother us.

I always try to spark a dialogue with my audience as soon as I can. If people can comment on my presentation, they begin to internalize the message; they make it their own. They also signal to their peers that they're engaged. They become my agents of impact. The distance between me and my audience is minimized, and so we can move forward together.

Assume the Persona of a Communicator

What does *communication* mean to you? If you think it's the sharing of information, you're only fractionally right. It is also the transfer of feelings, the expression of one's identity, the building of community and the creation of the future. There is no such thing as "just the facts." Everything is infused with the persona of the communicator.

Persona is the public face that we project to the world. It is what other people believe us to be. Our authentic self and private life are hidden from view. Our persona is the kind of person our words and actions have shaped us to be in other people's minds. And when it comes to communication, perception is reality.

Warning: if your persona diverges dramatically from the real you, it will crumble. The truth will come out. Nothing stays in the closet for very long. Every day, I watch the drama of fake identities come undone. Whatever I say to you in the next few pages is predicated on a consistency between who you are and who you profess to be. You cannot communicate like a champion unless your whole self comes out to play.

You cannot communicate like a champion unless your whole self comes out to play.

Megan Rapinoe is the poster child for communicating like a champion. As the captain of the 2019 World Cup–winning US women's soccer team, she was voted MVP of the tournament. Together with her teammate Alex Morgan, she scored the most goals; she also got the most penalties. When the pressure was most intense, she was given the job of putting the ball in the net. It's no coincidence that, at 34, she was also one of the oldest players on the team. The kind of poise she possesses comes only from repeated exposure to the heat of battle.

In addition to her prowess on the field, Rapinoe has led the women's soccer team's fight against pay disparity versus men. She is also an LGBTQ2+ activist. She and WNBA star Sue Bird were the first openly gay couple to appear on the cover of ESPN *The Magazine*'s iconic "Body" Issue. "It's important for people to come out. Visibility is important," Rapinoe told ESPN's Jemele Hill in a June 25, 2018, interview. "It's important for there to be a first one on the cover. Just in terms of the culture and society, someone has to do it."

Her persona is outspoken, brash, charismatic, fearless, team-oriented, civic-minded, athletic, disruptive and joyful. She knows exactly what she stands for in other people's minds. She means what she says and she says what she means. She doesn't shy away from controversy. She uses her bully pulpit as a world champion to promote equality issues at all levels. Her short-cut, purple-tinged hair and her impish smile complete her image as an iconoclast and disruptor.

The Communication Checklist of Champions

Let's unpack the elements that enable Rapinoe to communicate like a champion. There are 14 actions that make up the Communication Checklist of Champions. For each action, I invite—*encourage*—you to Make Your Breakthrough, in an exercise that follows each item. Some might require just thinking and reflection, but other breakthroughs will require some action and *reaction*. That sounds like a lot to ask—but each action will help take you to a higher level of your training.

1. You must be a champion of something

You cannot communicate like a champion if you're not a champion. You must have achieved preeminence in your field, or you must be passionately committed to a cause—or both. I can only write about being the Potentiator because I've achieved thought leadership status in this domain. I don't say this to impress you. I say it to impress *upon* you the need to develop your championship chops in the matters that mean the most to you.

MAKE YOUR BREAKTHROUGH

Develop Your Championship Chops

What are you a champion of? Define it. Share it. *Enhance* it.

2. Know your persona

What is the public face that you want to project to the world? What do you want people to believe you to be? What perception do you want them to have of you? Make sure the answer to these questions is consistent with the person who you believe yourself to be.

My persona is Magic Mike: the Motivator and Potentiator. I'm an impresario on my own behalf. I'm also a CEO co-pilot who enables leaders to fly at high altitudes. It's taken years of experience and experimentation for me to craft this persona, and I'm constantly fine-tuning it to fit changing circumstances—soliciting feedback, both positive and negative. I take great care of my persona because it's an integral part of my personal brand, which I depend on for a living.

I also vigorously promote my persona at every opportunity. That's not self-aggrandizement; it's just good business.

MAKE YOUR BREAKTHROUGH

Define Your Persona

What is your persona? Think about it. Write it down. Come back to it tomorrow. Revise it. Continue to craft it. Share it. Act it. Assess it. Amplify it. Make this a never-ending process.

---

3. Know your style

Your style is the way you express yourself to the world. It's the clothes you wear. It's the words you say. It's the gestures you use. It's the way you behave. It's the symbols associated with you. Rapinoe has an exuberant, athletic, dynamic style; I have an expressive, energized, demonstrative, humorous style. Be conscious of your style, because other people are. Watch yourself on video; listen to yourself on audio. In the future, people will see or hear you as many times by proxy as they do in person. Your style is the ticket to the show. It's what makes you unique and unforgettable.

Your dress says as much about you as any other non-verbal cue. I choose bespoke suits to help package my appeal as the Potentiator. I keep Tom Ford's advice in mind at all times: "If you dress for success, it is important to be convinced of the outcome."

How do you want to be described? What are your signature words? What is your trademark look? If we watched you or listened to you, what would we think and how would we feel about you? In fact, how would we think or feel about ourselves?

MAKE YOUR BREAKTHROUGH

Express Your Style

No need to write it down. Just make it conscious. Try it on. Act it out. Refine it until it feels exactly right for you. Repeat.

4. Know your outcome

Every conversation, presentation or call has a desired outcome. There is a reason people have given their time to the event: they want a higher return on it than they would have earned elsewhere.

Begin with the end in mind, then repeat it over and over again. In this book, I've engaged you in one long conversation. At the start, I told you exactly what it means to be the Potentiator, and each Potentiator Practice has drilled down into a separate area of mastery. Like a chorus in a song: *repeat, repeat, repeat.* But do it in a way that reaffirms why someone else chose to give you their time in the first place.

Before I make any recommendations to clients, I ask them four questions: What does success look like to you? What do you hope to achieve through this program? What do you want your people to get out of it? And how will we actually measure its impact?

MAKE YOUR BREAKTHROUGH

Clarify Your Outcomes in a Way that Clarifies Them for Others

At the start of every important meeting or call—beginning with your next one—make it clear to your clients or colleagues what success looks like. Then keep referencing it to accelerate your way there.

---

5. Have a roadmap

It's one thing to know where you're going; it's another thing to know how to get there. One person's small step is another person's giant leap. A lack of directions can lead to hesitation and anxiety. The hardest parts of any journey are the beginning, middle and end; the only easy part is *afterward*. As the Potentiator, you get people started. You pull them through the plateaus. You push them over the finish line.

It's like using Waze. You indicate your current location. You indicate your destination. It gives you alternate routes. It tells you how long each one will take. It indicates where the bottlenecks are. As conditions change, so do the routes. It makes good on its promise to outsmart traffic together with you.

This book is my roadmap for you. I have clearly expressed the end in mind, guiding you through each of the Potentiator Practices. But I also know you'll go deeper on the Potentiator Practices that are most valuable to you—creating even more opportunities to help you play at your best.

Champion communicators take their audience on a journey. They establish a connecting theme or a through line that ensures continuity and engagement. The through line in this book has been the constant reference to becoming the Potentiator and creating breakthroughs with others. That's my discipline against detours or superfluous detail. Whatever else happens, keep it tight. Err on the side of succinctness. Attention is a mercurial commodity—it can come or go at any time, especially online.

MAKE YOUR BREAKTHROUGH

**Build a Set of Directions to Lead
People Where They Need to Go**

Identify the journey you're taking others on. Establish
your connecting theme. Define your set of directions. Set the milestones of success. Test-drive your
message. Get feedback. Adjust and adapt. Keep
course-correcting as you go.

6. Connect others to their purpose

In the hurly-burly of everyday life, it's easy for people to
become reactive and forget their purpose. The need to make
a living can supplant the need to make a difference. Communicating like a champion reminds people of what makes them
champions. It lifts them out of the swirl. It reminds them
what they are here for. That's why we are sometimes literally
brought to tears by something we've seen, heard or read. In
that moment, we're connected to something that's worth living for, fighting for, stretching for.

Then the challenge becomes follow-up. Success is a result
of following through on your commitments after the mood in
which you made the commitment expires. That's the role of
the Potentiator: to goad, cajole, prod and pull people toward
their goals, no matter the obstacles.

The most valuable role to play in anybody's life is to be
that person who brings out the best in them. By conditioning
others to see you as their direct link to their better self, you
ensure that they always want more of you.

All of this assumes that you know what's most important to others in the first place. You do your homework. You understand their dreams, and you help express them. You use the language of their desire. That's how you make them want to do what they have to do.

MAKE YOUR BREAKTHROUGH

**Identify What Is Most Important
to Others in the Conversation**

Discover their "why." Embed it in your communication with them. Make it explicit. Keep reminding them of it—especially when they lose sight of it. Position yourself as the person who will help them live it. Do this for the next person you talk to. Then *keep* doing it.

---

7. Strip away the inessentials

Get rid of anything that interferes with your message. Be focused: streamline your delivery so every element enhances your impact. Whatever you say or write must contribute to your desired end in mind. Your audience must be able to see, hear and feel your consistency.

Every sentence or statement is an investment in your persona. While you always need to be experimenting with new approaches, keep your eye on the prize. If it gains traction, try it again; finesse it until it becomes a strength. If it doesn't work, discard it immediately.

One of the most common mistakes that people make is their indulgence in junk phrases or "fillers" as part of their everyday language. These are phrases such as "you know," "et cetera," "and so on," "I feel like I want to say" or "it kind of..." They are cotton-candy words that don't mean anything. They are fluff that get in the way of substance. In the future, when you are tempted to use one of your favourite doesn't-mean-anything phrases, *pause*. Be *silent*. Even use an "ummm" if you're thinking of the best words to use.

The same goes for your non-verbal language. Avoid fidgeting or engaging in gratuitous gestures. When you're speaking, make your hands your grammar. Keep them by your sides. Or hold them lightly together in front of you, fingers touching, at the ready. Use them decisively as exclamation marks. Turn them palms up as a question mark. Never point a finger at someone. Rather, point your whole hand toward them—with your palm facing inward, and all five fingers pointing at the other person.

MAKE YOUR BREAKTHROUGH

Identify Your Junk Words and Gestures

Be aware of when you're using them. Then get rid of them. Replace them with silence, appropriate pauses and strong movements. Stay the course on this one. A lifetime of habits won't go away easily. Note your improvements. Celebrate yourself. Then focus on the next conversation.

8. Speak their language

Nobody ever says, "I like you because we've got big differences." Instead, we say, "I like you because you're speaking my language." We like people who are like us. We respond to cues at an unconscious level that trigger our emotions. Words are packages of meaning that move us into action—either toward or away from others.

If you want to create immediate rapport, use the other person's words and phrases. Paraphrase what they've just said. Show your compatibility with their vocabulary. Express your appreciation of the way they portray the world. Use phrases like "I like the way you put that"; "When you said [X], that really resonated with me"; "I want to make sure I've got this right: You said..." "Huh! That's fascinating. I never thought of it that way before. Let me repeat that..."

MAKE YOUR BREAKTHROUGH

Speak Their Language

Listen for other people's key words and phrases—especially the ones that signal their joy and excitement. Then use them discreetly in your communication with them. Develop your audio-sensitivity to each person. Treat every conversation as an opportunity to become even more adept at this skill.

9. Talk louder and slower

Champion communicators ensure that others can hear their every word. They are loud, but not intrusive. They don't shout. They simply say it like they mean it. They make declarations, not just announcements. They inspire, not just inform.

The less confident people are, the softer they speak. They almost don't want to be heard because they're not sure that their words are worth hearing. So, they underemphasize their key messages. Anxiety or nervousness permeates their delivery. They just want to get off the stage and out of the spotlight. Their audiences are left feeling dissatisfied and uneasy because they don't quite know what they should be taking away from the presentation.

Confidence sounds like it has earned the right to be there. It stands out. It rings true. It seems real. It draws you to it because it's how you want to feel: certain, assured, at ease. Confidence earns your trust. You don't have to struggle to hear it or understand it. It demands your attention and interest. It's slightly louder than normal, but not overly so.

Confidence moves at a deliberate, considered pace: not too fast, but not too slow. It allows you to process each thought before moving on. It doesn't feel rushed. It just feels right. If you want to communicate with confidence, talk about 20 percent louder than you would normally be comfortable with.

Not only will you be more audible, you will also avoid going too fast. You cannot talk loudly and rapidly. A higher volume forces you to enunciate your words. If you have a naturally deep voice, use it. The deeper your voice, the greater your perceived gravitas. If your voice is naturally higher pitched, be aware of modulating your timbre: that's the natural quality and character of your voice.

For example, James Earl Jones may have the deepest voice in show business. He is the voice behind "This is CNN." He uses his voice like the finely tuned instrument that it is. Jerry Seinfeld, on the other hand, has a higher-pitched voice. He uses it to hype his humour. He always appears to be on the verge of his trademark pseudo-hysteria. Anderson Cooper's voice is more nuanced. He uses it to maintain his trademark unbiased stance as a mediator between guests with divergent points of view.

Marilyn Monroe's voice had a legendary huskiness. It was an instrument of seduction. Meryl Streep's voice, on the other hand, is smooth and soothing, with a gentle strength. She hypnotizes viewers into attention.

Each one of these global celebrities is (or was) acutely aware of their vocal impact on others. They are trained in the art of connecting with others. They have their own unique sound. It's the same with me. I try to pack as much enthusiasm as I can into every word I deliver—knowing that if I can capture people's hearts, their heads will surely follow.

Talking louder and slower is especially important when it comes to virtual communication. You stand a much greater chance of being heard and listened to. Your assumed authority will transcend the static and distractions. It could be the one quality that truly sets you apart, because the webcam tends to make people tentative and uncertain. I often watch people losing their composure the longer they speak. They even say things like, "Now I'm blabbering" or "I don't know if I'm being clear" or "I don't even know if that makes sense."

See the webcam as your ally. Use your imagination to visualize the people that you cannot see agreeing and endorsing your point of view. Remember to be own best avatar. Expect

Confidence
sounds like it
has earned
the right
to be there.

to feel a little awkward every time, but radiate your authenticity even when you feel inauthentic. Be comfortable being uncomfortable—because the only thing that really matters is how you make other people feel.

MAKE YOUR BREAKTHROUGH

Discern Your Unique Sound and Tempo

Identify the qualities of your voice that will move others into action. Ask people you trust for their feedback. What effect does your voice have on them? What about your pace of delivery? Record yourself speaking. Then play it back. It's normal to be uneasy with the sound of your own voice at first. It doesn't sound the way you hear it in your head. Keep listening so you can get used to it. Always be intentional in your speaking.

---

10. Lean in

Champion communicators tilt in the direction of their audiences. They pivot toward them. They walk to the edge of their stage. If they're in a chair, they thrust their head and their torso toward others. They show their level of interest with their entire bodies.

In the virtual realm, this poses unique challenges. How do you lean in while staring into a computer camera? How do you bring the audience closer to you? The answer is simple but it isn't easy: find those ways of recreating intimacy or closeness online. Get the best external microphone to make sure your voice is clear and warm-sounding to the audience. Get a ring light to cast a warm glow on yourself while speaking. Use a high-quality webcam to ensure your visual clarity and sharpness. Make sure the webcam is at eye level so you're not looking down on anyone. Position yourself so that people can see you from the torso up. And finally: look directly into your webcam, emote and use gestures—just as you would in a real-life setting.

Perhaps the greatest challenge of virtual presentations is looking and sounding "all-in" when you can't see your audience. That's when you need to pretend that you're directly in front of them. See people listening to you in your mind's eye. Imagine your impact to the upside. Ask yourself, "How can I make this experience even *more* rewarding for them?" If you stumble or fumble, it will just make you more human. Acknowledge your authenticity and move on.

Whether you're speaking in person or on camera, you need to show that you're totally committed to the conversation. Signal your involvement with a posture of full engagement. Others will raise their game in direct proportion to your participation. They want to feel like others care as much as they do. People want permission to play full out. Give it to them.

Above all, show that you relish being in front of others. Whether you're an introvert, extrovert or ambivert, make others feel vicariously delighted to be with you. Smile or laugh where appropriate. Show your passion in a way that's right for you and them. Actually tell them how much you're enjoying being with them. Express your gratitude for their time and attention. Reassure them that this has been a great investment of your time and make them think the same thing. Be the reason why people believe in themselves.

> **MAKE YOUR BREAKTHROUGH**
>
> **Practice Leaning In**
>
> In your next meeting, consciously demonstrate that you're all in, all the time. Imagine you are watching a video recording of the meeting. Make sure it shows someone who is more engaged than anyone else in that meeting.

11. Inspire while you inform

The data doesn't mean anything without the meaning behind it. Content is key, but it's how you communicate that turns it into currency. You must turn big data into anecdata. Your story must stir your audience's hearts and capture their imagination. They must feel emboldened to take on their bogeymen.

No matter what your style or your job, you are first and foremost a motivational speaker. That means that people should be motivated to do something as a result of talking with you. It doesn't require verbal pyrotechnics, but it does require a conscious intent and ability to move people into action.

One size doesn't fit all. Inspiring while informing means adapting your approach to different audiences, both verbally and non-verbally. I will talk to firefighters in a very different way than I will talk to actuaries, for instance. In the former case, I will make it more vivid, direct and even physical; my examples and metaphors will focus on rapid response, crisis resolution and mastery of intense emotions. In the latter case, my delivery will be more clinical; I will demonstrate how my insights positively influence longer-term consequences and will appeal to their logic as much as to their leaps of faith.

In order to inspire anyone else, you must be inspired. Remember why you're there in the first place: you're the Potentiator. You're there to help others play at their best. You need to do whatever it takes to uplift your spirit. It isn't easy, but it is essential. Your *will* must be bigger than your *won't*. If you want to communicate like a champion, you need to always be on—no matter what else is going on.

The next time you're in conversation with someone, ask yourself how you're coming across to them. Think about the degree of excitement you're sparking in them. Consider how you could make this meeting the highlight of their day. Be their keeper of the flame.

Often, people will tell me before I stand up to speak that they are excited to hear me. Or they tell me about someone they know who is a fan. Or they will share a memory from a time they heard me before. Simply knowing that I have supporters in the audience inspires me to play at my best. The smallest actions can move the needle in the right direction.

MAKE YOUR BREAKTHROUGH

Assess Your IQ—Your Inspiration Quotient

Intentionally talk and act in a way that uplifts the spirits of others. Observe the impact that you're having on them. Play to the different psyches of the people in the room. Choose your top three stories and learn to tell them well. Get feedback from your confidantes about the effect that you're having on others.

12. Promote the people around you

We're all addicted to CRAK: Compliments, Renown, Admiration, and Kudos. CRAK is the real currency of success. Paying someone a compliment for their extraordinary contribution, helping them build renown in their field, expressing admiration for their achievements, applauding their efforts in person and online—these are the direct lines to people's reciprocal support for you.

Whenever I hear that someone else is promoting me, I feel a reciprocal surge of wellbeing and gratitude toward them. I am surprised and delighted in equal measure. I feel validated and valued by the people who matter. It's the unexpected antidote to all the unpleasant things that may have happened to me that day. That's why I praise my stakeholders in public, as part of either my live presentations or my content. It costs nothing and it means everything to the person being celebrated. I believe in my network and I want it to show.

The following phrases are like elixirs to other people's ears:

* The thing you do extremely well is . . .
* I really admire you because . . .
* I have to give you credit for . . .
* All kudos to you for . . .
* You're a great example of . . .
* We were blown away by your . . .
* You inspire us with your . . .
* We will wholeheartedly recommend you to . . .
* We loved your . . .
* You made a massive difference . . .

It's curious, but whenever I promote the people around me, they thank me for my generosity. They appreciate my willingness to help them win. They act as though I've expended precious resources on their behalf. The truth is that I was simply practicing what I preach. In the spirit of full disclosure, I was *also* boosting their predisposition to promote me even more strongly in the future. It's called enlightened self-interest.

MAKE YOUR BREAKTHROUGH

Practice Promoting Others

In the next three days, compliment three people a day. Catch them doing something right and authentically deserving of the compliment. Express your admiration in a way that is natural and reflective of their achievements.

---

13. Improvise with ease, especially when it's hard

The hardest part of any speech isn't the part that you've rehearsed and repeated many times. It's the dialogue that follows. It's how you handle the difficult moments created by puzzling audience responses, or questions asked by people who may not even want you to succeed. Hecklers of all kinds could be part of the mix.

Our best moments can be camouflaged as crises. Paradoxically, that's when the audience is most engaged. Problems are a deviation from the expected norm. They make the experience interesting. They introduce drama and the potential for conflict. They remove our artifice and reveal the real person beneath it all.

I'm used to vocal cynics or skeptics in my meetings. It's easier for people to sound smart when they're criticizing someone else's point of view or highlighting why something won't work. Sounding too optimistic can get you branded as naïve. There are also people who relish their role as the naysayers or troublemakers in the organization. How you handle them earns you either the respect or contempt of the group.

Here are eight simple steps for improvising with ease, especially when it's hard:

1 Prepare in advance for the kinds of questions or objections that could be made by detractors. But be careful about shoehorning your response into a prepared statement so it doesn't sound disingenuous.

2 Pause to look at the person. Be silent for a couple of seconds.

3 Thank the person for their participation. Tell them that you appreciate their willingness to express their point of view.

4 Express your understanding of why they would have that point of view.

5 State that other people may also share that point of view.

6 Acknowledge that their point of view may be as valid as the point of view that you're espousing.

7 Use the words "That said" to segue into data points that reaffirm your statements. Share examples that develop your argument even further.

8 Where appropriate, use humour to endear yourself to the audience and show your complete lack of rancour or anger toward the other person.

MAKE YOUR BREAKTHROUGH

Improve by Practicing Improvisation

In your next three meetings with clients or colleagues, prepare to improvise with the eight steps outlined above. Put yourself out there. Experiment with different approaches. Don't worry about getting tangled up. Just tango on.

---

14. Be eloquent with your emails

Eloquent is defined by the Oxford Dictionary of English (third ed.) as "being fluent or persuasive in speaking or writing; clearly expressing or indicating something." Do your emails perform that function for you? Do they communicate your desired intention? Do they leave people feeling informed and appreciated? Or just dazed and confused? If I could judge you based only on your emails, what would my conclusions be?

Emails are the formal letters of the digital age. They are the electronic representation of your voice and style, instantly visible to thousands with a press of a button. They demonstrate your respect for others (or lack of it). They can be long or they can be a single word, but they must be appropriate to the message you wish to send. Careless emails signify that you couldn't care less. No matter how busy you are or how many emails you're sending, make sure that every one is the most eloquent one you can send in that moment. Just like your live delivery, be guided by the style and preferences of the people you're corresponding with. Some people want lengthy emails and others like it short. Use your good judgement to decide how much time you're willing to invest in the exchange. And *thoroughly* read the emails to which you're responding: when it comes to asynchronous communication, reading is the new listening. Demonstrate that you've paid attention to the cogent details. Motivate others to read your emails when their inbox is overflowing.

Here is a checklist of five essential elements to guide the way you craft your emails:

1 **Make your subject line compelling.** If the heading doesn't grab attention, the email may not get read.

2 **Structure your message appropriately.** Keep it simple. Lead with the objective of the message. Provide context. Have a specific call to action.

3 **Repeat the first name of the recipient throughout the email.** Personalized emails are far more likely to be read.

4 **Make your content readable.** Avoid long blocks of copy. Use headings and bullet points. Employ spelling and punctuation checkers to prevent basic errors.

5 **Follow up with grace.** Give people time to respond. Follow up within 48 hours if you don't hear from them. Don't make people feel guilty for not responding. Simply resend the email with a different heading. If they're important to you, make sure you respond to others within 24 hours.

> **MAKE YOUR BREAKTHROUGH**
>
> **Review the Quality of Your Emails—and Raise It**
>
> Take an honest look at your emails and ask yourself whether you're doing yourself and others justice. Use software to check your punctuation. Think about the response that you're generating from others—is it the kind of reciprocation you want? Read the emails of people you enjoy corresponding with and those you don't. Consider how others would categorize *you*.

Navigating the Boundaries of Personal Space

There used to be a playbook for how to communicate in different cultures. In Mediterranean cultures, for instance, people historically would touch each other a lot more than they do in North America. Straight men hugged and kissed each other, usually on the left cheek, then on the right. Women did the same.

With the pandemic, however, socially distanced communication styles became the rule—in all corners of the globe—and many time-honoured cultural rules went out the window. Will the double-cheek kiss return? How about the 10-second handshake?

In the future, we all might become a bit more like the English and the Germans—who have always preferred to guard their personal space—or maybe even the Japanese, who tend to avoid touching strangers altogether (saving that intimacy for close friends and family).

Still, it's hard to believe that we won't gradually want to return to *some* contact, in *some* parts of the world, as a way of showing our appreciation and gratitude toward each other. As someone who has worked in 72 countries, I have discovered that appropriate contact—a light touch on the shoulder or arm, at the right moment—can make *all* the difference in my communications. Touch cannot be applied remotely—and frankly, I think we will once again welcome these small gestures. They are physical reminders of our proximity to each other. They also suggest a level of intimacy and equality that is the hallmark of a healthy relationship.

That said, when in doubt, *do not touch*; learn to respect personal boundaries and appreciate cultural boundaries, especially in this post-pandemic age. But when the moment calls for it—when a "new normal" has established itself— remember that physical gestures present a unique opportunity to brand yourself as someone who cares enough to have literally *reached out*.

Turn the Jitters into Jet Fuel

I deliver over a hundred keynotes or workshops annually, and people often ask me whether I get nervous before my presentations. The answer is *yes*. Some days are worse than others. There is always something going on beyond the impending presentation. There are always unwelcome thoughts that trespass on my psyche. There is always something that isn't quite right. For me, all that internal noise is normal.

Pre-talk jitters are constantly present. Every presentation is independent of the one that preceded it. For the audience about to receive it, it is the only one that matters. Many of the attendees are seeing me for the first time; they may never see me again. Sixty to ninety minutes will define their perception of me for the rest of their lives. They will become mobilizers or detractors.

When I don't feel the jitters, I'm complacent. I take the opportunity for granted. I'm flying too high on hubris or ego. I'm not crediting the opportunity with the significance that it deserves. My adrenaline isn't flowing. I am going into the presentation not firing on all cylinders. It usually doesn't go well.

I have learned to turn the jitters into jet fuel. Nerves sharpen my senses. They force me to engage in my pre-presentation rituals that take me into the zone. I visualize my success. I repeat my mantra over and over again, a translation of an ancient ayurvedic maxim: "Oh Lord, grant me the power of divine speech."

I take deep breaths. I warm up my facial muscles with smiles and grimaces. I loosen my tongue with tongue-twisters like "Peter Piper picked a peck of pickled peppers" and "You know New York, you need New York, you know you need New York." I stand proud, thump my chest, pump my fist and declare, "Yes!" By the time I get onto the stage or in front of the webcam, I'm ready to rumble.

The Art of the Big Ask

You can't get what you don't ask for. Life's treasures are reserved for the people who know how to request them. The knight in shining armour is a medieval myth that never existed in the first place. No one (other than your mom) is as

You honour others by requesting big things from them.

committed as you are to your success. And yet, many people have huge difficulty in making the big ask of others.

Part of the problem is the fear of rejection. Another part is our cultural conditioning that we shouldn't be making the ask. A third part is the uneasiness that comes with doing something that we hardly ever do. A fourth part is the fear of making the other person feel awkward. Sound familiar?

As the Potentiator, you make big asks of others because you believe in their capacity to grant your requests. You honour others by requesting big things from them. You appeal to your stakeholders' higher nature while you challenge them to grant your requests. You also know how to make the big ask by doing three things:

1 Establish a background of relatedness. Show how you and the other person are connected. Articulate your common purpose.

2 Make your request appear to be an invitation to an opportunity for the other person to get what they want.

3 Enable the other person to grant your request by outlining exactly what they need to do.

By way of example, if I am trying to persuade a prospect to invest a sizeable sum in one of my coaching programs, I make the request as follows: "Both of us are committed to being the benchmark of excellence. You are acknowledged as the best in your industry, and I am acknowledged as the best in mine. If you bring me into your organization, I will endow your salespeople with the confidence and knowledge to endear themselves to their customers. They'll win the business that's currently eluding them and have fun doing it. Increases in market share and revenue will follow. Here is the roadmap that outlines the way forward..."

MAKE YOUR BREAKTHROUGH

Make the Big Ask

In the next week, choose one person that you can honour by making the big request of them. Then make it. Don't worry about whether or not the request is granted. Be satisfied with merely having made the request. In the next month, make a big request of three more people. Then make it a habit.

5

The Fifth
Potentiator Practice
Cultivate Close
Connections

You can face the future only because of the people who have got your back.

MIKE LIPKIN

I N JULY 2019, I received the kind of phone call that I pray for. It was from Diane, the vice president of sales at a Fortune 500 company.

"Hi, Mike, we are in the early stages of planning an 11-city roadshow for the end of the year. We would like your input on the most compelling theme and content for our clients," she said in her voicemail. "Given the deepening disruption to our industry, we think you're well qualified to give our delegates the insights and inspiration they need. We have scheduled a meeting with our senior leadership team at the end of next week, so we would like to talk with you as soon as possible."

Of course, I responded immediately and won the assignment—one of my biggest that year. Ever since I first started working with Diane in 2002, I have cultivated our relationship. I have reached out to her with a regular cadence of emails, calls and meetings. I have also helped guide her through some difficult moments, including a professional hiatus after her position was eliminated as a result of a corporate merger in 2013.

Diane, along with many other well-placed people, is the lifeblood of my business. She is the reason I got the nod ahead of hundreds of equally qualified competitors. By the same token, I have lost many assignments because my competitors have their own "Diane" going to bat for them. No matter what business you're in, you're in the business of connecting with people who have the power to make a difference *on your behalf*. Ironically, you need to cultivate your strongest connections to your weakest ties. Why? Because your closest acquaintances talk to the same people as you do. They move in the same circles. They connect with the same opportunities. It's the people on the outer edges of your network that introduce you to a whole new realm of possibilities. I talk to Diane only once or twice a year. But her path intersects with people I would never otherwise encounter. She is a fan, not a friend. And I've learned to keep my friends close but my fans closer.

During the pandemic, the importance of cultivating close connections was brought into stark relief. It was a time of tremendous turbulence. Within weeks of the first lockdown, I lost several clients who thought of me only as "the live guy"— they were not interested in pivoting to a virtual format for my presentations. But I also brought in a whole new generation of clients who *specifically* came online because of the pandemic. And perhaps most importantly, I was able to deepen my relationship with a third of my existing clientele who wanted to evolve our arrangement to virtual *because* we had already established a close connection. They sought familiarity in a strange new reality.

Cultivating close connections is a combination of touch and technology. We can have thousands of Instagram followers, Facebook friends and LinkedIn connections—but we can only cultivate close connections with about 150 people in any given year. They are the ones to whom we cannot just send blanket emails. They need more than just form newsletters or generic videos. They need our personalized attention and customized acumen. They are the ones with whom we need to go deep, not wide. Sometimes, the connection is a one-off and sometimes, as with Diane, it can last decades.

People are social animals. Among the hundred-plus questions asked in the annual Environics Research Social Values Survey, the following one—on close connections—gets the same reaction, year in and year out. It is an expression of the universal need for intimate human connection. Over 90 percent of respondents in the US and Canada say that they keep in touch with a small number of people with whom they share deep and warm relationships.

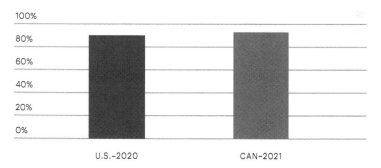

% Agreement:
"I like to keep in touch with a small number of people with whom I share deep and warm relationships."

SOURCE: *Environics US Social Values Survey, 2020; Environics Canadian Social Values Survey, 2021 (© 2021 Environics Research, all rights reserved)*

It's easier to create breakthroughs with others if you cultivate close connections with them. That's how you get past the outer walls into their inner sanctums, especially in a post-Covid world where the walls are built higher. Furthermore, the more discerning the person, the greater the height of their walls. Who we allow to get close to us is one of the most important decisions we can make. Social trespassers are not permitted.

We're All Lonely Now

A 2020 study by the global health services firm Cigna found that 61 percent of US adults reported feeling lonely in 2019. That's up from 54 percent in 2018—and post-pandemic, I believe, the numbers will be even higher. "We're all lonely now," novelist Olivia Laing wrote in a *New York Times* column days after lockdowns began. "Social distancing is vital, but that doesn't make it easy." We have literally been through a prolonged period of social isolation. No matter how many people are in our inner sanctum, we will feel entirely alone more often than ever before.

Along with loneliness come anxiety and feelings of profound distress. According to a study by the Environics Institute for Survey Research, between April 2019 and December 2020, the proportion of Canadians rating their mental health as excellent or very good fell from 53 percent to 38 percent. The proportion saying their mental health is fair or poor increased from 21 to 31 percent over the same period. And, according to the June 14, 2021, issue of *Time* magazine, during the pandemic, rates of depression and anxiety soared to 40 percent of all US adults, quadruple previous levels.

It isn't likely to get easier any time soon, but cultivating close connections can make us better at dealing with whatever comes next.

Dunbar's Number

In the 1990s, Robin Dunbar, a British anthropologist, came up with Dunbar's number. This is actually a series of numbers that comprise the maximum scope of human interaction. He maintains that 150 is the maximum number of people we would call casual friends—say the number of people you would invite to a large party. The next step down is 50, perhaps the people who you would invite to a milestone birthday gathering.

Then there's an inner circle of 15: your close confidantes. The most intimate Dunbar number, five, is your close support group. On the flip side, your acquaintances group can extend to 500. The limit is 1,500 people for whom you can actually put a name to a face.

Over the past 20 years, social researchers have found Dunbar's numbers to be remarkably consistent. No matter how broad our social networks become, we can maintain only 150 to 200 stable personal connections at any one time. It's a simple function of a finite resource called *time*. It takes a certain temporal investment to build social capital.

The more connections you have, the less time you can invest in developing each one. CRM (customer relationship management) software can provide you with the insights and key data points, but it cannot replace the personal calls and meetings that need to be made.

Who are your 150 people with whom you're cultivating close connections? And what are you doing to enter and stay in their inner sanctums?

Every time you meet somebody, they should feel energized by that interaction.

The Most Valuable Time Is Actual Face-to-Face Time

Pre-pandemic, I was on the road all the time—because, let's be honest, there simply is no substitute for breaking bread with a client or looking into their eyes. While we've all had to adjust to more texts, emails and calls—and Zoom chats replacing the real thing—there is little doubt that the thirst for getting back together is strong. As much as we've been seduced into the ease and wonder of virtual engagement, we still crave actual face-to-face time because of the relative scarcity of in-person encounters.

Wall Street investment bankers Goldman Sachs and JPMorgan Chase started urging their staff to get out and visit corporate clients as soon as it was safe to do so. David Solomon, Goldman's CEO, and Jamie Dimon, the JPMorgan chief, both led from the front. Dimon told his people, "If you need to use a plane to go see a client, use it. There are no excuses." Dimon himself flew to Paris and Rome to meet French president Emmanuel Macron and Italian prime minister Mario Draghi, respectively.

JPMorgan even staged a contest where bankers were awarded points for visiting senior clients. The bank recorded more than a thousand total in-person meetings for June 2021. They were often the first to see clients in person since the pandemic hit. The more things change, the clearer it becomes: the most valuable time you'll get is face-to-face.

In an ironic twist, "social" media—and our increasing reliance on it—may actually be shrinking our ability to cultivate close connections. Clicks and swipes are not touches. Blocking, disconnecting and unfriending don't require the negotiation, communication or closure skills that are part of real life. And while we're all conditioned to respond to the vibration or ping of incoming alerts, we're ambivalent about being seduced by the sender. It's like eating a candy or indulging in a snack that you didn't need but couldn't resist. No matter how good it is, you know you would have been better off without it.

As we return to the next normal, and in-person meetings become routine, ensuring that these encounters are *not*, in fact, routine will be crucial to cultivating close connections. We don't want banal conversation. We don't have patience for futile face-to-face meetings. We won't accept personal contact that leaves us unmoved. Technology may have enabled our survival during Covid, but it hasn't replaced the craving for extraordinary experiences. Every time you meet somebody, they should feel energized by that interaction.

The more surrogates there are for physical presence, the more physical presence is appreciated. If you want to fan the fire, you need to fire up your fans. Every contact with one of your 150 close stakeholders must be an extraordinary experience, in ways big or small. As with Diane and me, the contact can be only a few calls or meetings per year, but *every one* must be memorable. If you get it right, each one of your stakeholders can influence the 150 members of their network on your behalf, in addition to their likes and comments on social media.

Paradoxically, the velocity and volume of so much digital interactivity makes personal connections even more impactful. The vast majority of our touchpoints are superficial exchanges of information or trivia. They are transactional, not transformational. No one's life is ever changed by a tweet, text or post. At best, it attracts our attention for an instant before evaporating into the ether.

That's why truly memorable interactions are so consequential. They are the peak experiences that we remember in a sea of noise. The time between experiences is less important than the intensity of the experience itself.

According to an article by Anne-Laure Fayard, John Weeks, and Mahwesh Khan in the March–April 2021 issue of the *Harvard Business Review*, the physical office will become primarily a culture space, providing workers with a social anchor, facilitating connections, enabling learning, and fostering unscripted, innovative collaboration. It will promote what the psychiatrist Edward Hallowell calls "a human moment." This is a face-to-face encounter that allows for empathy and emotional connection.

And listen to this: the same article stated that the Human Dynamics group in the MIT Media Lab found that face-to-face interactions outside formal meetings were the best predictor of productivity.

The office of tomorrow will be characterized by three elements: it will be designed for human moments. It will be customized by technology. And it will be managed to encourage connections. In other words, it will be a place where people *want* to come—because it's indispensable to their growth and wellbeing. Other people's happiness at work will be directly linked to your mood and behaviour. They will vicariously experience your emotions. When you show up in person, you need to bring the heat, no matter what the weather.

No Blockers Allowed

There is an opportunity cost to every call. Every meeting is a forfeited chance to meet with someone else. The time you invest in your conversations is an investment that must yield the highest return because you're never getting it back.

Being the Potentiator maximizes your ROR (Return on Relationships). When you're someone's superhero, that's a deep and strong connection. It's not just making one sale or doing one deal—it opens up an enduring stream of lucrative possibilities. Creating breakthroughs with others is good business. It enables you to do it for the love *and* the money. Passion and profit go hand in hand—but only if the right people are on your side.

The 150 people with whom you choose to cultivate close connections must be people who can maximize your impact. Each one must represent a gateway to opportunity that is worthy of your efforts. In other words, you need to cultivate mobilizers and advocates while you avoid blockers.

I touched briefly on mobilizers earlier. They are the geese who lay the golden eggs. They are the people who are respected and admired within their organizations. You can find them at every level. They are both the formal and the informal leaders. They have a reputation for helping others get things done. Mobilizers are your greatest social assets—but they can also be the toughest people to connect with. They may be the ones with the most objections to your offering. They can appear to be skeptical, opinionated or just downright difficult. They're intentionally testing your content and character before they champion you to their organizations. Treat every interaction with them as an opportunity to prove your mettle.

Advocates are one step removed from mobilizers. They support you but they don't command the same status in their own organizations. Their recommendations lack the gravitas of mobilizers but they can still put you on an organization's radar. Advocates can put you in front of mobilizers. They can also accelerate the decision-making process in your favour, but they are not the decisive factor. Meanwhile, blockers are your *bêtes noires*. They are the ones who prevent you from getting any kind of traction. They may not have malicious intent; they just don't like you or your offering. Trying to convert a blocker is like Don Quixote tilting at windmills—and you have better things to do.

Don't confuse mobilizers with blockers. Mobilizers test you because they want to see if you have the right stuff. Blockers simply set you up for failure. You can tell the difference by the quality of the questions and responses you receive. Mobilizers will recognize your worth once you pass muster. Blockers either make the process ever more painful or just go silent on you.

If you realize you're being confronted by a blocker, minimize your interaction with them. Double down on the advocates and mobilizers around them. Don't get mad—that would be exactly what blockers want you to do. Get the win or move on.

MAKE YOUR BREAKTHROUGH

Weave Your Network of Mobilizers and Advocates

In the next two weeks, identify 10 mobilizers and advocates with whom you need to cultivate close connections. Identify how you can help potentiate

their success. Then call them. Follow up with an email.
Come back to them every quarter.
Make the pursuit of mobilizers and advocates a
core discipline.

Let Me Tell You a Story about the Power of Empathy

Empathy is the connective tissue that binds us together. It is the ability to sense the emotions of others and vicariously experience them without other people explicitly telling you what they feel. Even the people in your inner circle won't automatically tell you what they really feel. They need you to make it easier for them. They need an invitation to be transparent. If you can demonstrate that you "feel" them, they will open up.

It's an act of reciprocity: if others sense that we get them, they are far more likely to get *us*. However, it's easier to be empathetic than it is to actually express our empathy in a way that convinces them. If someone just nods their head and says, "I understand how you feel," you may not fully believe them. Worse, you may even feel like they're patronizing you. It's only when they can communicate their empathy that a genuine connection is made.

So, just how intrigued, interested and motivated is the average person to take the perspective of the other—to be in their place, walking in their shoes? Less than you think. The next graph suggests that only about a quarter of the general population claims to like walking in the shoes of other people—to really feel what they feel. When you consider that at least some of this 25 percent are probably responding to the question in a socially desirable manner, the real number is likely lower. In a world where there is a general deficit of empathy, the empathetic are outliers.

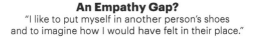

An Empathy Gap?
"I like to put myself in another person's shoes and to imagine how I would have felt in their place."

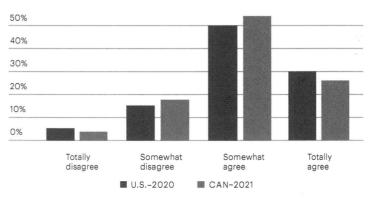

| | Totally disagree | Somewhat disagree | Somewhat agree | Totally agree |

■ U.S.–2020   ▓ CAN–2021

SOURCE: *Environics US Social Values Survey, 2020; Environics Canadian Social Values Survey, 2021 (© 2021 Environics Research, all rights reserved)*

The main reason so few people are committed to empathy is that it demands a substantial investment of time, focus and energy. It requires a willingness to experience the pain and struggle of others without being burdened by it. It can be uncomfortable to walk a mile in their shoes.

Without empathy, though, it's impossible to be the Potentiator. And during the Covid-19 pandemic, it really was the empathetic leaders who rose to the top; they were the ones who demonstrated that they truly understood the humanity of their employees, co-workers or clients. They brought a higher level of compassion to everything they did, every Zoom meeting they hosted. After all, it's only when a common zone of shared trust and perspective is established that you can truly help someone play at their best, even in the most difficult circumstances.

In my conversations with clients, they share that one of their biggest challenges is establishing empathy with others in a virtual setting. They say that they cannot read the body language, get a "feel of the room," or use all the non-verbal language that would be available to them in a physical meeting. These difficulties are real but they are not insurmountable. In some ways, it can be even easier to express your empathy virtually. You can express your shared frustration or awkwardness. You can communicate your deep desire to put people at ease while exciting them to be on the call. You can invite them to express their point of view by calling them in, not calling them out. Whatever happens, you can assure them that a virtual meeting with you is both a safe and enjoyable space. Then, of course, you have to walk your talk.

Here are five ways to create empathy with others—no matter who they are or where you find them.

1. Do Your Due Diligence on Them

Cultivating close connections with people is like entering into a contract. There is a reason you want to cultivate a close connection in the first place. As the Potentiator, your mission is to help them play at their best. In exchange, you want a return that can be measured in social or economic capital.

Just as a lawyer or investor is expected to do due diligence on their interests, you need to do your due diligence on the people with whom you want to get close. The data is all around you, but it's not enough just to know about the person;

you need to know about their context. Who are their influencers? What changes are they confronting? Who are they running with? How can you position yourself as a thought leader in their world? It's especially important to know about the world of your mobilizers and advocates.

Only a tiny minority of people take the time to do due diligence on the people with whom they're endeavouring to cultivate close connections. The rest don't have the inclination or don't believe they have the time. They're not curious enough to want to find out more. The irony is that it's never been easier to glean the essential details that define others' lives. All it takes is a few fundamental facts that you can leverage in the conversation to activate deeper dialogue. I'm always amazed by how favourably people respond to me when I reveal that I've researched them.

The obvious source of personal data is social media. But that source needs to be overlayed by research into the realities, hopes and fears that characterize their worlds.

I have done my due diligence on you—my reader. I know your greatest commercial challenge is differentiating yourself in a sea of cutthroat competition. I know that you understand the power of contribution at the highest level; that your role is that of enabler of other people's progress; that you're strongly committed to personal growth; that age isn't relevant to you; that you're already successful and you want to achieve even more; that you're anxious and excited about the future in equal measure; that you back yourself, you back others and you're giving others reasons to back you.

I've tailored my message to people like you because you are where the power, the opportunities and the money are. How am I doing?

2. Accept Them as They Are

In its essence, empathy is a total, unconditional acceptance of other people as they are, not how you would like them to be. In a sense, it entails becoming that person, getting inside their head and imagining what it must be like to live in their skin. It must be accompanied by a sense of wonder and fascination. No half measures allowed.

When you accept people totally, you begin to take on their characteristics. You assume their stance, their way of speaking, their energy and their mindset. They feel your alignment with their way of being. They begin to relax. Then they begin to share things that they would withhold in a tense state.

I will warn you that accepting people as they are can be excruciatingly hard. There are all kinds of triggers within you that will be set off by other people's appearance, language and behaviours. There will be temptations to judge and criticize. Your patience will run short. You will feel the need to apply your worldview to their situations. That's when you have to remember what it takes to be the Potentiator. You are there to create breakthroughs with others. If they feel that *raison d'etre*, you'll cultivate a close connection. If they don't, you won't. So what will that take for you?

Valuable questions to ask are: What happens if they're right? Why is their approach valid? What do they need most from me right now? What's the best thing about them? Why should I adore and admire them? How do I show my adoration and admiration? What questions can I ask that will get them to open up even more?

3. Understand Their Values

A value is the measurement by which people evaluate what is important to them. It's how they prioritize the application of their time, money and energy. By demonstrating that you understand people's priorities, or even that you want to understand their priorities, you open up a channel of connection.

People will tell you whatever you need to know if you listen closely enough to what they're saying and how they're saying it. Display an authentic curiosity to know more. Use phrases such as, "I'm curious to know more about what's really important to you" or "I hear what you're saying. Does that mean...?" or "I can see why that could be important to you. Can you help me understand it even deeper from your point of view?"

You can go even further by articulating what you've heard: "So what you're saying to me is..." or "What I heard is that..." or "Let me make sure that we're aligned; am I right that you believe..." Say it out loud so others know they've been truly listened to.

4. Relish Their Presence

Nobody wants to feel like a nobody. No one wants to be taken for granted. I dread meetings with people who don't seem to want to meet me. One of my greatest social fears is that others will find me boring. I shut down when I sense I'm being judged. Discomfort and unease block my willingness to share.

On the other hand, I open up to people who I believe are open to me. I love being fêted, especially if it's by people I hold in high regard. I play at the level of my audience. If they bring the heat, so will I. Their happiness ignites mine. Empathy is a mutual gift that must be continually celebrated or it dries up. So, in every meeting, compliment the other person. Flatter them like you mean it, because you do. You can't "fake it till you make it." You can only unleash your genuine joy.

Anything less is disingenuous. If you don't have an authentic affection for the people you're with, you can never become their Potentiator. When you say, "I'm pleased to meet you," or "It's a privilege to be here," it must be true for you. The simple act of letting people know you're glad to be with them can be the impetus for them to give more than they otherwise would have.

So seize every opportunity to verbalize your delight at being with others—but always make sure it's coming from your heart. And when you receive a compliment, accept it with relish. Demonstrate your pleasure and pride. Don't stop at a simple thank-you. Add a little anecdote about how you acquired the asset being complimented. And lob a compliment back in return. Research shows that compliments light up the brain's reward system and accelerate rapport.

So—I want to commend you for making it this far. You're showing your commitment to becoming the Potentiator. Thank you for your resolve and your passion for this work. It means a lot to me.

5. Go First and Go Deep

If you want to embolden people to risk more of themselves than they usually would, you have to lead by example. You have to share secrets or confidences that you would normally keep close to your chest. You need to strip away the façade that you would normally present to others.

If you want others to reveal themselves to you, you need to reveal key parts of yourself first. As you've read in this book, I have opened myself up strategically. I have exposed facts about myself that I believe to be appropriate to the mission of this book: helping you become the Potentiator. There is nothing gratuitous here. Just the relevant facts.

The closest connections occur when, by sharing your narrative, your story becomes *other people's* story. This is a more frequent phenomenon than you may expect. There are universal themes that we all experience. Names, places and dates may change, but the human journey is remarkably consistent: loneliness, not belonging, abandonment, powerlessness, futility, unfairness, cruelty, confusion, discovery—to name just a few themes that are common to us all. As Oprah Winfrey has said, "The struggle of my life created empathy—I could relate to pain, being abandoned, having people not love me."

The phrase "Let me tell you a story" is guaranteed to hook people's attention for at least 60 seconds. But when you tell it, you need to make sure it's relevant, moving and short. Then allow the other person to tell *their* story. If they're not immediately forthcoming, keep going with patience and compassion. Eventually, they will open up.

And here's an action that you can take in every meeting— virtual or face-to-face: be the first person to ask a question or make a comment when the host asks for it. Don't let them twist in the uncertainty of whether or not anyone is going to respond. They will never forget your generosity. And you will make it easier for others to follow.

Become an Outsider-Insider: "Wow! How Do They Know That?"

If you ask most people, they would say they don't feel like insiders, or part of the club. And paradoxically, it's the people who are succeeding on most business metrics who most often feel like outsiders.

They have what Jim Collins, an authority on business leadership, calls "productive paranoia." They are hyper-vigilant to the threats around them, including not being "in the know." They're highly sensitive to cues that indicate their status in their organizations and their awareness of key data points.

Even as the Potentiator, you cannot give what you do not have.

The art of being the Potentiator is increasing other people's confidence in their powers, especially when they doubt themselves. It entails transferring both the knowledge and self-belief that enables people to play at their best. But even as the Potentiator, you cannot give what you do not have. You need to penetrate your client organizations at a meaningful level.

Then you need to engage like someone deeply entrenched in the organization. You have to embody the traits of its most successful members. It's part play-acting and part skills-mastery. Most importantly, it's about blurring the lines between being an outsider and being an insider.

I call it becoming an "outsider-insider." It's when you elicit a response from clients that says, "Wow! How do you know that?" You come across as someone who understands the client's business as well or better than they do. Achieving this goal is not as difficult as it may seem. There are many similarities between industries and organizations. You have to know just enough to give the impression that you know *much more*. You need to make yourself temporarily indispensable. Becoming an outsider-insider happens one person, one contribution, one win at a time.

MAKE YOUR BREAKTHROUGH

Become an Outsider-Insider

Here are 14 ways to brand yourself as an outsider-insider. Review them all. Then choose three actions that you believe will give you the greatest traction with your key stakeholders. Make them part of your everyday regimen. Assess yourself on their effectiveness. As you move forward, try others. Discover your own ways to become an outsider-insider. Create your own checklist. Make this discipline a never-ending part of your personal renaissance.

1 Scan the media for comments or articles by industry leaders. Summarize the key messages and forward them to your clients with your personal observations.

2 Codify your expertise by posting your points of view. Create your own how-to guides and playbooks. Hire the talent to help you get it done. It will be the best investment you can make.

3 Anticipate your clients' needs by reaching out to them with recommendations before they reach out to you.

4 Introduce your clients to other key players in their space. Leverage your network to help expand theirs.

5 Get out into the marketplace. Spend time in your clients' world. Share your observations and recommendations for enhancement.

6 Maximize your exposure to leaders throughout the organizations that you serve. Gain their trust through the quality of your conversation and your grasp of their business.

7 Preserve the confidentiality of your communication but advertise the range of leaders with whom you're working.

8 Volunteer to give more than is expected of you.

9 Use simple tools like online surveys and video conferences to build your own knowledge base. Then package your insights with a catchy headline and actionable follow-through.

10 Reframe your clients' point of view through the lenses of your experience. For example, leverage your exposure to other industries to highlight the things they aren't examining, but should be.

11 Take time out to evaluate your own presence and contribution. Ask yourself, "If I were them, would I listen to me? How can I become even more interesting and relevant to them?"

12 Label yourself as the Potentiator. Stake your claim as a game changer. Pass the point of no return so you can't turn back.

13 Keep refuelling your passion for the grind so you keep your pedal to the metal.

14 Turn your clients into your personal board of directors. Once you've made the deposits into the credibility account, you can make withdrawals. Ask them for their advice and guidance about who else you can serve.

Don't Be Manic, Be Talismanic

Are you feeling lucky today? Are you wearing your favourite suit, shirt, necklace, shoes or socks? Did you go through the rituals that prepare you for a successful presentation or contest? Did you speak to the people who inspire you to play at your best? Are you working with your favourite client or colleague? Did you whisper a silent prayer to the great salesgod-in-the-sky to multiply your mojo? Did you listen to the music that stirs your heart and mind to greatness?

No matter how rational we humans think we are, there is a part of us that believes in the mysterious, the magical or the supernatural. There is a superstition that runs through all our thinking. How else can we explain all the amazing coincidences that have shaped our lives? How can we explain the good fortune that we've enjoyed when others, just as skilled as we are, have fallen short? What are the reasons why we just bumped into opportunity and narrowly avoided disaster? Why has serendipity played such a large role in our success? How did the best and the brightest find their way into our lives? How did we find ourselves in just the right place at just the right time so often?

Being seen as lucky is a powerful asset. As Dwight D. Eisenhower said, "I'd rather have a lucky general than a smart general. They win battles."

Luck is the name that we give to success when we don't fully understand it. It's a composite of many factors. Some of them may be divine gifts that we received at birth. Some may be results that we've worked hard to achieve. Some may simply be because we've made more connections and taken more chances than our peers. And some may be karmic payback for good deeds. Whatever it is, *lucky* is an adjective that you want people to apply to you—especially if you become renowned for spreading your luck around.

The Cooler is a 2003 film about an unlucky individual who, in casino parlance, is called a "cooler." William H. Macy plays a casino employee whose mere presence at a gambling table causes a streak of bad luck for other players. I'm talking about the *opposite* of a cooler. I'm talking about a talisman.

A talisman is someone whose presence causes others to succeed. When they are around, others achieve results that they believe they would not have achieved without the assistance of the talisman. They believe this person provides them with the skills, resources, connections, courage, inspiration, energy or insights to do things they otherwise would not have done. They link their good fortune directly to the intervention of the talisman.

I call this the *positive outcome effect*. Instead of simply correlating the outcome with the presence of a talisman, people assign the cause of the outcome to the talisman. Sometimes, they can track the outcome to a specific contribution by the talisman. Other times, they fabricate the outcome through their imagination. Either way, the talisman becomes integral to their wellbeing. Then it becomes self-fulfilling. Their triumphs become accretive. As long as the talisman is in their corner, they take on monsters that would otherwise have cowed them into inaction.

Not every talisman is a Potentiator. But every Potentiator is a talisman. They have earned their reputation as the cause of others' good fortune. Sometimes, Potentiators are too humble for their own success. They are the unsung heroes and heroines. They live according to the dictum that actions speak louder than words, so they don't publicize their contributions. In my book, however, words amplify actions. The more people you can tell, the more people you can benefit—and the more people can become your champions.

Miguel is a testimony to the power of a talisman. He has been one of my largest clients for over a decade. He is a senior leader of a global logistics company and, every year, he invests tens of thousands of dollars with me. On many occasions, his board members have challenged him on the spend, especially in the face of economic headwinds—but on every occasion, Miguel simply tells them that I am his insurance against underperformance.

Ever since he began working with me, Miguel has outplayed his industry. The line between what I really give him and what he *believes* I give him was erased long ago. I have been woven into Miguel's narrative. While I'm always pushing the envelope for him, I'm also deeply appreciative of his superstition.

I have a quick checklist to gauge your status as a talisman:

- When people see your number on their call display, do they take your call?

- Do they associate you with opportunity?

- Do they look forward to talking with you?

- Are you a guaranteed highlight of their day?

- Are they inviting you into important meetings?

- Are they consistently investing in your contribution because they believe it's so valuable?

People vote with their time and money—either *for you* or *against you*.

If You Want the Fruits, You Have to Water the Roots

The laws of commerce are not always analogous to the laws of nature. Sometimes it can take years for seeds to germinate— and sometimes it can be almost instantaneous. I cultivated some clients for years before they rewarded me with their business. On other occasions, I have connected with clients at exactly the moment they were looking for my offering. The truth is that I expect both outcomes; I am prepared to pursue the former and am delighted by the latter.

Cultivating close connections is an all-season, every-year, never-let-up kind of activity. Pessimism is not an option, and neither is complacency. Being the Potentiator means that you always take 100 percent responsibility for growing your relationships. Resentment, resignation and blame are never options. When you succeed, you enjoy the dividends of your endeavours; when you lose, you lick your wounds, learn what didn't work and carry on. The gestation period is longer for some relationships than for others. Often, nothing went wrong. The process simply had to run its course. If you stay engaged, you can win. If you quit, you automatically lose.

Embrace a Philosophy of Philanthropy

Philanthropy literally means "love of humanity." It is demonstrated by the gifts of your time, capital or effort to a designated cause. A philosophy of philanthropy is the continuous search for ways to express your love of humanity by sharing your most valuable resources (time, capital, energy) with causes that are meaningful to you. Sometimes the act may be as simple as an online donation to a cause championed by one of your stakeholders.

Or it could be an undertaking into which you pour your heart, mind, body and soul. One of the best things that others can say about you is that you're a giver; one of the worst things they can say about you is that you're a taker. Givers get credit when they need it most; takers are hung out to dry. A philosophy of philanthropy earns you kudos from the people who are crucial to your success. It makes them want to be with you. It also motivates them to follow your lead and find their own philanthropic focus.

In my case, I deliver pro bono workshops and keynote addresses to non-profit or professional organizations like the United Way and the Toronto Regional Immigrant

Employment Council, as well as to high schools and universities across Canada. The opportunities I have generated through my philanthropic activities always pay off in actual revenue and network development. It's an oxymoron: selfish generosity. I give to get. It's that simple.

MAKE YOUR BREAKTHROUGH

Give to Get

In the next two weeks, decide on your philanthropic focus. Then publicize it. Put your name on it. Make sure that others know how you're making a difference. Post your commitment to the cause. Talk about it whenever you can. Give enough to really feel it. It's when you don't think you have the time or resources that you need to give them to others.

The Greatest Ability Is Dependability— Don't Just Be Trustworthy, Be Faithworthy

Trustworthiness means that others can depend on you. It's table stakes. It means that you won't let people down. You'll meet the required standards. You'll show up on time. You'll be responsible. You'll play your part. You won't be a source of other people's anxiety or uncertainty. You'll demonstrate a level of consistency that maintains status quo.

Faithworthiness means that people can *believe* in you. It's a game changer. It means that you can be relied on to produce an outstanding performance *every time*. You'll swing the odds in favour of your stakeholders. You'll redefine the part. You'll be the continual source of others' inspiration. You'll lift them up to the next level—whatever that is. If you're around, things are likely to go very well.

If you want a disproportionate reward, you need to make a disproportionate investment. Being faithworthy requires a willingness to take on the responsibility of being known as the come-though person. It's a mindset that regards pressure as a privilege. If people believe in your ability to expand their power and effectiveness, they will choose you over your competition every time.

Come Through in the Crucible Moments

After almost 40 years of researching human motivation, I have discovered that people want to believe in the goodness of others. For example, in the Environics 2019 annual study of Canadians' social values, nearly two-thirds of respondents stated that from the first instance, other people should be assumed to be trustworthy rather than untrustworthy (64 percent vs. 36 percent). Over half of the respondents (52 percent) said that they counselled such trust in others with "no hesitation."

I've also discovered that people believe what they want to feel. Call it confirmation bias, wishful thinking or just plain naiveté. It's a deep need to feel confident in other people's desire and ability to help us succeed. That's why betrayal is such a searing emotion. It reminds us that our trust is not always justified. People don't always act with our best interests in mind. It's a double-whammy: we feel not only *alone* but also *threatened* by people we thought were on our side.

In their landmark *Harvard Business Review* article from September 2002, Warren Bennis and Robert Thomas brand the experiences that shape leaders as "crucibles," after the vessels medieval alchemists used in their attempts to turn base metals into gold. They state, "For the leaders we interviewed, the crucible experience was a trial and a test, a point of deep self-reflection that forced them to question who they were and what mattered to them. It required them to examine their values, question their assumptions, hone their judgement. And invariably they emerged from the crucible stronger and more sure of themselves and their purpose—changed in some way."

In the 20 years since Bennis and Thomas wrote those words, the number of crucible moments has increased exponentially. Every day, we face micro-crucible moments punctuated by larger ones. Sometimes, they're thrust upon us and sometimes we take them on intentionally because that's where our contributions are most needed. It's precisely in the crucible moments that being fanatically faithworthy really matters. Potentiators resolve never to be the reason someone loses faith in others.

The highest praise you can receive is someone else's "SOS" in their crucible moment: if you come through for them then, they will be lifelong resources for you to draw on. *But* if you don't respond effectively, you become just another disillusionment in a disappointing world. Either you're potentiating greatness—or you're sowing cynicism. Remember: BFF—Be Fanatically Faithworthy.

MAKE YOUR BREAKTHROUGH

Review Your Crucible Moments

Identify and review three crucible moments for you from the past year. Evaluate your performance against the "faithworthy" standard. Assess what you could have done to raise your game. Ask yourself these three questions: In the past year, what situations or experiences rocked me to my core? What changes did I make as a result? How did they, or how could they, make me more faithworthy? Consciously take those actions in your next crucible moment. Evaluate, assess, act. Repeat.

Master the Art of the Apology

Only in the movies does love mean never having to say you're sorry. In real life, cultivating close connections depends on how effectively you express regret if and when things go wrong.

The absence of an apology can signal a lack of caring for someone else's distress or disappointment. It can also signal ignorance about the consequences of your actions. Love is relative. There is the deep romantic love that you have for your partner. There is the deep filial love that you have for your family. But the vast majority of our relationships may not be characterized by a deep love. It's more like affection, trust, interdependence, affinity, wellbeing, affirmation, rapport or harmony. The status of all those relationships is far more precarious. They can be shaken by a single mishap, wrong word, rumour or omission.

Like death and taxes, mistakes are inevitable. The best intentions and preparations can go awry through life's vagaries and vicissitudes. In the chaos or the crisis, it's easy for others to misinterpret the reasons for shortfalls or deficits. We all go through rough patches, when we feel like we're under siege. Even the smallest misstep can feel temporarily crippling, especially if we believe others don't care—or, worse, are acting antagonistically toward us.

An elegant apology is like a salve to our spirit. It soothes our disquiet. It could be a simple "I'm so sorry to make you wait" that we hear from a waiter. Or a basic "My bad" as someone admits when they've erred. Or a straightforward "You're absolutely right—I'm at fault here" when a disconnect occurs.

A well-delivered apology restores our sense of dignity. It validates our sense of fairness. It makes us feel like we're important. It reaffirms our view of reality. It takes away our anger or frustration at not being seen or heard. In many cases, it can be the difference between drifting away or being drawn back toward the other person.

Great apologies share four characteristics:

1 They're authentic.

2 They express unqualified responsibility for the actions that were taken.

3 They acknowledge in unambiguous terms that the action was wrong or inappropriate.

4 They are a declaration of contrition or remorse.

For example, if you said something that upset someone else, you could simply state, "I should never have said that.

I was out of line. I'm so sorry to have upset you." Then your behaviour needs to be commensurate with your mea culpa.

Close with Grace

To everything there is a season. The closest connections are miraculous. They can start in the most unlikely ways. A simple glance, sound, note, fragrance, phrase or touch can ignite decades of passion. One moment, they're nothing. The next moment, they're all that matters.

I love to ask people who are in a professional or personal partnership how they met. Often, they'll smile in a dreamy kind of way. Or they'll shake their heads as if to say, "You won't believe it." Then they'll share their story, punctuated with chuckles, sighs, smiles and happy silences. Their partner will usually contribute with a contrasting perspective along the way. The narrative ends with both partners looking at each other with a renewed sense of mutual appreciation.

Close connections can end just as suddenly as they start. The context shifts. People evolve. They lose their trust and attraction for each other. Or they find it somewhere else. It's time for them to move on. You can't bring back that loving feeling if it's gone, gone, gone.

That's when it's time to close with grace. As the Potentiator, you provide others with the closure they need. You communicate why the connection is lost or the deal didn't happen. You enable the other person to make sense of the ending and carry on with dignity. You don't just leave them hanging. You understand and acknowledge the depth of the other person's shock or dismay. While you can't always give

As the Potentiator, you provide others with the closure they need.

others what they want, you do your best to give them what they need.

We've all experienced the debilitating silence that can follow the termination of a relationship. One day, we're someone's best friend or most valuable service provider. The next day we're totally out of favour. Often, we don't even know the reason for the abrupt change of sentiment. That's the real source of pain.

I endure these moments more than many. Something I say, or even the way I say it, can alienate others. Overnight, I go from hero to zero. It hurts to be cancelled—but it's an inevitable part of the game. I just make sure that I'm not the one doing the cancelling. No ghosting allowed, especially when a simple email or phone call can save someone's dignity or assuage their self-doubt. It will also set you free from your conscience and minimize your regret when you look back on your actions.

MAKE YOUR BREAKTHROUGH

Get Complete with People You've Fallen Out With

Think about three people you need to tie up loose ends with. Think about what they must be feeling about their experience with you. Think about what you could say to them that would wrap things up with class and compassion. Think about how you feel being incomplete with them. Think about how you will feel about yourself after you take these actions. Then do them. Now would be a good time.

The woods are lovely, dark and deep, But I have promises to keep, And miles to go before I sleep.

ROBERT FROST

Epilogue

O N MAY 27, 2018, Mamoudou Gassama—a 23-year-old undocumented immigrant from Mali—climbed four storeys of a northern Paris building to save a four-year-old child dangling from a balcony. The child had been left alone and somehow made it over the railing. Christened Spider-Man on social media, he became an overnight celebrity. Two days later, he met with French president Emmanuel Macron at the Élysée Palace, where he was awarded "the honour medal for courage and devotion"—and received his residency permit the next day (in September 2018, he became a French citizen). Just as important, Gassama's heroic gesture became an example for all citizens and a rallying cry for the support of undocumented immigrants.

Gassama told the press that he noticed the child dangling from the balcony around 8 p.m. while walking with his girlfriend on the street below. "I didn't think about the floors or the risk," he said. "I climbed up to save him, *voilà*."

It took Gassama just a few seconds to save a life, become a hero, get his papers and make a statement on behalf of thousands of people. But it took him a lifetime to build the character, instinct and skills to perform the task. When the moment appeared, he was ready.

Get ready for your **Gassama moment.** You know it's coming in some form or another. It may save a life. It may save other people's time, money and effort. It may change the way people think. It may change the way they interact with others. It may make a difference to one person or it may make a difference to the world. It doesn't matter. As the Quran, Surah 5 verse 32, says, "If anyone saves a life, it shall be as though he had saved the lives of all mankind." And to paraphrase the Talmud, "Whoever saves one life, saves the world entire."

You won't be Spider-Man . . . You'll be the Potentiator!

Someone out there you haven't even met is depending on you to keep promises you haven't even made yet. Be prepared to meet the person and make the promises—even if you don't know how to keep them. Growth and integrity are a function of figuring it out, no matter what it takes. As you go looking for the solution, the solution comes looking for you. Whatever you look for is what you tend to find.

Aspire to Something You May Never Achieve

Have you ever been so good in a meeting that you amazed yourself? You say the thing that needs to be said, when it needs to be said, how it needs to be said. The words flow out of you in a silken stream. You conjure up the insights and spread them like magic dust. You show how deeply you've been listening and how intimately you understand other people's aspirations. They pause in admiration, acknowledging your brilliance, expressing their appreciation and reciprocating with a breakthrough of their own. You look around you in wonder that you are the source of such wisdom.

It's sublime when it happens. My question is: How often does it happen? Is it a rare lightning strike? Or is it a frequent phenomenon? Are you even noticing when it does? Do you give yourself credit? And are you consciously trying to make it your norm?

In karate, becoming a black belt means that you have reached the level of sublime skill. You have progressed through white, yellow, orange, green, blue and brown belts. You have invested more than five years in active training. But within a black belt, there are 10 *dans*, or degrees of skill. Being a first dan means that you've achieved your "beginning degree" in the journey toward the tenth dan—a qualification that very few practitioners ever achieve. The point is not the realization of the tenth dan but the aspiration and actions to achieve it.

By coming this far, you've achieved your beginning degree. Congratulations! Take a bow. And take a break. Savour your achievement. Celebrate it with your peeps. Share a breakthrough or two with them, together with your favourite beverage. Listen to yourself transfer your insights and inspiration. Observe your impact. You know that you truly know only when you can help others know.

Then get to work. The road to mastery is paved with great intentions that are passionately executed, one Potentiator Practice at a time. Know Your Game. Build Robust Resilience.

Grow Courageous Creativity. Communicate Like a Champion. Cultivate Close Connections. Use the Personal Reflections pages at the end of this book to record your experience.

This is Mike Lipkin, and it's been a thrill creating breakthroughs with you. Let me know how this book is helping you become the Potentiator by sending an email to mike.lipkin@ environics.ca. I'm only as good as the difference you make. Let's go do it!

The Vocabulary of Victory

Advocates: One step removed from mobilizers. Advocates support you but they don't command the same status in their own organizations.

Authentic actor: Who you are when you express the best part of you while you play your part.

BFF: Be Fanatically Faithworthy. Being unreasonable on others' behalf by helping them burn their excuses and become victors, not victims, of their circumstances.

Blockers: Your bêtes noires; people who prevent you from getting any kind of traction.

CARE: Clear, Authoritative, Reassuring, Empowering.

Chutzpah: Shameless audacity; not being afraid or embarrassed to say or do things that may shock, surprise, dismay or annoy others.

CRAK: Compliments, Renown, Admiration, Kudos.

Dunbar's number: A series of numbers that comprise the maximum scope of human interaction.

Dynamic deniability: The refusal to grant disempowering things the power to ambush your wellbeing or positivity.

Faithworthiness: Earning other peoples' belief in you because you can be relied on to produce a goosebumps-inducing performance every time.

FLAP: Finish Like a Professional.

Gassama moment: An action that may save a life, or change the way people think and interact with others. It may make a difference to one person or it may make a difference to the world.

Gumption: The ability to decide the best thing to do and then doing it with energy and determination.

Mobilizers: People who are your champions waiting to happen; your greatest social assets.

Neutrals: People who are indifferent to your charms and flaws.

Outsider-insider: Someone who blurs the lines between being an outsider and being an insider. Someone who understands the client's business as well or better than they do.

Personal principles: Our internal truths that shape our mindset and behaviour.

Positive outcome effect: When people assign the cause of the outcome, instead of the correlation with the outcome, to the presence of a talisman.

Potentiator: Someone who creates breakthroughs by helping others play at their best. A superhero whose superpower is to turn other people into superheroes.

Powerful promise: The opposite of under-promising; a promise that captivates others and enrolls them in your cause.

Pre-suasion: The ability to move people in a direction that persuades them to give assent to a message before they encounter it.

Robust resilience: A constant state of conditioning that enables you to turn any surprise into a breakthrough.

ROR: Return on Relationships. It's not just making one sale or doing one deal—it's an enduring stream of lucrative possibilities.

RRR: Robust Resilience Response. A way of interpreting any situation that empowers you to carry on with even greater vigour.

Self-savvy: The ability to understand the intersection of your principles, your effect on others and the role you must play.

Situational sensibility: An appreciation of the complex influences that are shaping the future.

Slump buster: A mantra, declaration or action you can take to forget the last defeat and focus on the empowering move that will propel you and others in the right direction.

Talisman: Someone whose presence causes others to succeed.

TUNA: Turbulence, Uncertainty, Novelty, Ambiguity.

Acknowledgements

FIRST AND FOREMOST, I want to thank my wife for motivating me during this literary marathon. Without her pushing me through my procrastination, I would never have completed this book.

I thank Dave Jamieson, chief scientist at Environics Research, for his extraordinary guidance along the way. His fingerprints are all over this book.

I thank the hundreds of clients whose insights and experience formed the raw material for this book. They were my Potentiators every step of the way.

I thank Jesse Finkelstein and her amazing team at Page Two for turning my thoughts into this spectacular publication. I would especially like to thank the designer, Peter Cocking, for another masterpiece, James Harbeck and Matt O'Grady for making their editorial magic with my original manuscript, and Rony Ganon for making it all happen.

Finally, I thank my higher power for aligning the stars with my endeavours to make this miracle real.

Notes

Introduction

Here are just four of the almost 9,000 words: "Updates to the OED," Oxford English Dictionary, public.oed.com/updates/.

As the poet Johann Wolfgang von Goethe allegedly wrote: This well-known quote is attributed to Goethe, but there is some debate online as to whether he originated it.

As Jim Loehr and Tony Schwartz wrote: "The Making of a Corporate Athlete," *Harvard Business Review*, January 2001, hbr.org/2001/01/the-making-of-a-corporate-athlete.

in the 2019 Environics Research Canadian Social Values Survey: Taken from the Environics Canadian Social Values Survey, 2019. (© 2019 Environics Research, all rights reserved.)

"I may be an isolated case": Christopher Reeve quoted by Jeffrey Kluger, "Against All the Odds," *Time*, September 16, 2002, content.time.com/time/magazine/article/0,9171,351207,00.html.

"She was, in a positive sense": Gina Kolata, "Kat Kariko Helped Shield the World from the Coronavirus," *New York Times*, updated September 24, 2021, nytimes.com/2021/04/08/health/coronavirus-mrna-kariko.html.

"It is already transforming for Covid-19": Gina Kolata, "Can Covid Research Help Solve The Mysteries of Other Viruses?" *New York Times*, April 17, 2021, nytimes.com/2021/04/17/health/long-covid-heart-research.html.

"Forget the last game, forget the last play": Ken Ravizza and Tom Hanson, *Heads-Up Baseball: Playing the Game One Pitch at a Time* (Chicago: McGraw-Hill Education, 1995).

"Coffee's for closers only": Alec Baldwin as Blake in *Glengarry Glen Ross*, directed by James Foley (1992; New Line Cinema).

"Champions win when": Billie Jean King quoted by Carol S. Dweck, *Mindset: The New Psychology of Success* (New York: Ballantine Books, 2006).

The First Potentiator Practice: Know Your Game

As the poet John Milton said: Goodreads, s.v. "John Milton Quotes," goodreads.com/quotes/6572140-the-mind-is-its-own-place-and-in-it-self.

"Acting for me has never been": Jessica Chastain to James Lipton on *Inside the Actors Studio*, episode 1, season 22, aired December 21, 2016, on Bravo, bravotv.com/inside-the-actors-studio/season-22/ep-1-jessica-chastain.

"What I feel onstage": Beyoncé Knowles-Carter interview in *Parade* quoted by Caitlin Johnson, "Beyoncé on Love, Depression and Reality," CBS News, December 13, 2006, cbsnews.com/news/beyonce-on-love-depression-and-reality/.

"Acting is not about being someone different," BrainyQuotes, s.v. "Meryl Streep Quotes," brainyquote.com/quotes/meryl_streep_369285.

"So if I asked you about art": Robin Williams as Sean Maguire in *Good Will Hunting*, directed by Gus Van Sant (1998; Miramax).

coined the term **pre-suasion**: Robert B. Cialdini, *Pre-Suasion: A Revolutionary Way to Influence and Persuade* (New York: Simon & Schuster, 2016).

when Jeff Bezos founded Amazon: Patrick Hull, "Be Visionary. Think Big.," Forbes, December 12, 2012, forbes.com/sites/patrickhull/2012/12/19/be-visionary-think-big/#214e1b0f3c17.

When Larry Page and Serge Brin founded Google: "About," company mission statement, Google, about.google/.

Walt Disney's purpose: Van Arsdale France quoted by Bruce Jones, "Mission versus Purpose: What's the Difference?" Disney Institute Blog, October 23, 2018, disneyinstitute.com/blog/mission-versus-purpose-whats-the-difference/.

The Second Potentiator Practice: Build Robust Resilience

According to a 2018 article by Luke Gartside: "How Dangerous is Surfing," *Wavelength* magazine, June 13, 2018, wavelengthmag.com/how-dangerous-is-surfing/.

At the 2018 Winter Olympics in PyeongChang: See olympics.com/en/ olympic-games/pyeongchang-2018; olympics.com/en/olympic-games/ pyeongchang-2018/results.

"A winner is just a loser who": Goodreads, s.v. "George Moore Quotes," goodreads.com/quotes/897172-a-winner-is-just-a-loser-who-tried-one-more.

"What does your brain need": David Eagleman, "Book Extract: 'The Brain: The Story of You', by David Eagleman," *Financial Times*, October 23, 2015, ft.com/content/3f5c647a-7768-11e5-a95a-27d368e1ddf7.

That's why, as Billy Joel sings: From the song "I Go to Extremes," by Billy Joel, track 4 on *Storm Front*, released as a single December 1989, Columbia Records.

As tennis star Roger Federer said: Simon Kuper, "Roger Federer: You Cannot Be Alone at the Top," *Financial Times*, June 28, 2019, ft.com/ content/7895fe14-9667-11e9-8cfb-30c211dcd229.

The Golden State Warriors congratulate: *Toronto Star*, June 17, 2019. See also Canadian Press, "Warriors Take Out Full Page Ad in Toronto Newspaper Congratulating Raptors," Global News, June 17, 2019, globalnews.ca/ news/5399627/warriors-full-page-ad-congratulating-raptors/.

Dr. Melissa Cugliari, a leading: Dr. Melissa Cugliari and Mike Lipkin, "Consciously Create Your Best Reality: The 10 Personal Best Practices That Are Scientifically Proven to Fuel Your Happiness, Health and Peace," Environics/Lipkin, pdf, mikelipkin.com/wp-content/uploads/ 2021/04/Consciously-Create-Your-Best-Reality-One-Pager_v5r.pdf.

Consider the winningest Olympian: Richie Allen, "Michael Phelps Workout and Diet," Muscle Prodigy, muscleprodigy.com/michael-phelps-workout-and-diet/.

Shouldice encourages patients: Shouldice Hospital, "Choosing the Right Surgeon to Repair Your Hernia!," shouldice.com/choosing-the-right-hernia-surgeon-to-repair-your-hernia.html.

"Victory awaits him who has everything in order": Roald Amudsen, *The South Pole: An Account of the Norwegian Antarctic Expedition in the Fram, 1910– 1912*, translated by A.G. Chater (London: J. Murray, 1913).

The Third Potentiator Practice: Grow Courageous Creativity

In their 2020 book *The Curious Advantage*: Paul Ashcroft, Simon Brown, and Garrick Jones, *The Curious Advantage* (Laïki Publishing, 2020).

To quote the band Nickelback: From the song "What Are You Waiting For?" by Chad Kroeger, Ryan Peake, Jacob Kasher, and Gordon "Gordini" Sran, track 3 on *No Fixed Address*, released November 14, 2014, Republic Records.

According to David Brodzinsky: Ruth Padawer, "Sigrid Johnson was Black. A DNA Test Said She Wasn't," *New York Times*, November 19, 2018, nytimes.com/2018/11/19/magazine/dna-test-black-family.html.

According to a 2020 Deloitte Global Millennial Survey: To download the survey, visit www2.deloitte.com/pt/en/pages/about-deloitte/articles/deloitte-global-millennial-survey-2020.html.

the most successful entrepreneurs tend to be middle-aged: Clive Thompson, "Who Are the Most Successful Entrepreneurs? The Middle-Aged," *Wired*, October 22, 2019, wired.com/story/most-successful-entrepreneurs-middle-aged/.

"In a strange kind of way": Glenda Jackson quoted by Parul Sehgal, "At 82, Glenda Jackson Commands the Most Powerful Role in Theater," *New York Times Magazine*, March 31, 2019, nytimes.com/2019/03/27/magazine/glenda-jackson-king-lear.html.

In a conversation with Toby Keith: Clint Eastwood quoted by Michael Hainey, "Clint and Scott Eastwood: No Holds Barred in Their First Interview Together," *Esquire*, August 3, 2016, esquire.com/entertainment/a46893/double-trouble-clint-and-scott-eastwood/.

"How old would you be": Taylor Robinson, "Satchel Paige: Age Is Mind over Matter," Bleacher Report, April 6, 2009, bleacherreport.com/articles/151960-satchel-paige-age-is-mind-over-matter.

To quote the great Springsteen: From the song "Racing in the Street," by Bruce Springsteen, track 5 on *Darkness on the Edge of Town*, released June 2, 1978, Columbia Records.

"We run the company by questions": Eric Schmidt to Jeremy Caplan, "Google's Chief Looks Ahead," *Time*, October 2, 2006, content.time.com/time/business/article/0,8599,1541446,00.html.

Meyers encapsulates the news of the day: Jonathan Ringen, "Seth Meyers Has Remade Late-Night Comedy for the Trump Era, While Also Being a Really Good Boss," *Fast Company*, May 22, 2019, fastcompany.com/90346137/most-creative-people-2019-nbc-seth-meyers.

"I think that the best thing we can hope": Meyers quoted in Ringen, "Seth Meyers."

During 2020, Perfect reported a 32 percent increase: Liz Flora, "Google and Snapchat Turn to Beauty Tech for AR Beauty Try-On," Glossy, January 26, 2021, glossy.co/beauty/google-and-snapchat-turn-to-beauty-tech-for-ar-makeup-try-on/.

They promise "Adventure Simplified"; Dipaola says it costs 30 to 40 percent: Visit autocamp.com for more information; Amy Farley, "How the Auto Camp Founder is Building the World's First Airstream Hotel Chain," *Fast Company*, May 22, 2019, fastcompany.com/90345832/most-creative-people-2019-autocamp-neil-dipaola.

"I have not failed ten thousand times": Thomas Edison quoted by Tim Leberecht, "3 Ways to (Usefully) Lose Control of Your Brand," October

28, 2012, TED Global video, 6:31, ted.com/talks/tim_Leberecht_3_ways_ to_usefully_lose_control_of_your_brand?language=en.

"To invent you have to experiment": Jeff Bezos, annual letter to Amazon shareholders, April 5, 2015, sec.gov/Archives/edgar/data/1018724/ 000119312515144741/d895323dex991.htm.

"It took me 15 years and 5,127 attempts": James Dyson, "Yes, It's OK It Took Me 5,127 Attempts to Make a Bagless Vacuum," *Globe and Mail*, August 11, 2014, theglobeandmail.com/report-on-business/careers/leadership-lab/yes-its-ok-it-took-me-5127-attempts-to-make-a-bagless-vaccuum/article19992476/.

Toastmasters epitomizes this notion: See toastmasters.org/about/all-about-toastmasters.

As the cartoonist Walt Kelly wrote: The phrase was actually first used in 1970 on an Earth Day poster, but Kelly famously used it in one of his comics and attributed it to Pogo.

"If you're still alive at the age of 50": Michael Merzenich, *Soft-Wired: How the New Science of Brain Plasticity Can Change Your Life* (San Francisco: Parnassus Publishing, 2013).

"seek first to understand": Stephen R. Covey, *The 7 Habits of Highly Effective People: Powerful Lessons in Personal Change* (New York: Free Press, 1989).

The Fourth Potentiator Practice: Communicate Like a Champion

It's important for people to come out: Megan Rapinoe to Jemele Hill in an interview, "Rapinoe on Body Issue Cover: 'Visibility Is Important,'" June 25, 2018, espn.com/wnba/story/_/page/espnwbodybirdrapinoe/wnba-sue-bird-uswnt-megan-rapinoe-debate-better-athlete-body-issue-2018.

The Fifth Potentiator Practice: Cultivate Close Connections

A 2019 study by the global health services firm Cigna: *Loneliness and the Workplace*, Cigna report, cigna.com/static/www-cigna-com/docs/about-us/newsroom/studies-and-reports/combatting-loneliness/cigna-2020-loneliness-infographic.pdf.

"We're all lonely now": Olivia Laing, "How to Be Lonely," Opinion, *New York Times*, March 19, 2020, nytimes.com/2020/03/19/opinion/coronavirus-loneliness.html.

According to a study by the Environics Institute for Survey Research: Andrew Parkin, "Mind and Body: Impact of the Pandemic on Physical and Mental Health," Environics Institute, June 2, 2021, environicsinstitute.

org/projects/project-details/mind-and-body-impact-of-the-pandemic-on-physical-and-mental-health.

during the pandemic, rates of depression: Joanne Lipman, "The Pandemic Revealed How Much We Hate Our Jobs. Now We Have a Chance to Reinvent Work," *Time*, May 27, 2021, updated June 1, 2021, time.com/6051955/work-after-covid-19/.

In the 1990s, Robin Dunbar, a British anthropologist: "Dunbar's Number: Why We Can Only Maintain 150 Relationships," BBC Future, bbc.com/future/article/20191001-dunbars-number-why-we-can-only-maintain-150-relationships.

"If you need to use a plane": Cara Lombardo and David Benoit, "Wall Street's New Rivalry: Who Can Meet the Most People in Person," *Wall Street Journal*, July 16, 2021, wsj.com/articles/wall-streets-new-rivalry-who-can-meet-the-most-people-in-person-11626453898.

According to an article: The piece is titled "Designing the Hybrid Office." See hbr.org/2021/03/designing-the-hybrid-office.

"The struggle of my life": Oprah Winfrey quoted by Lisa Messenger, *Life & Love: Creating the Dream* (Australia: The Messenger Group, 2015).

productive paranoia: Jim Collins with Morten T. Hansen, *Great by Choice: Uncertainty, Chaos, and Luck—Why Some Thrive Despite Them All* (New York: Harper Business, 2011).

"I'd rather have a lucky general": Dwight D. Eisenhower quoted by Charles Vallance, "Business Leaders Who 'Leave Nothing to Chance' Attract Bad Luck and Missed Opportunities," *Telegraph*, April 20, 2014, telegraph.co.uk/finance/comment/10777363/Business-leaders-who-leave-nothing-to-chance-attract-bad-luck-and-missed-opportunities.html.

"in the Environics 2019 annual study of Canadians' social values": Taken from the Environics Canadian Social Values Survey, 2019. (© 2019 Environics Research, all rights reserved.)

"For the leaders we interviewed": Warren Bennis and Robert Thomas, "Crucibles of Leadership," *Harvard Business Review*, September 2002, hbr.org/2002/09/crucibles-of-leadership.

Epilogue

"I didn't think about the floors or the risk": Translation of quote by Mamoudou Gassama in Aurélie Foulon, "Mamadou Gassama, le premier jour du reste de sa vie," *Le Parisien*, December 2, 2018, leparisien.fr/societe/mamadou-gassama-le-premier-jour-du-reste-de-sa-vie-02-12-2018-7959210.php.

Let's Start a Conversation

LET'S TALK about how I can help you and your team become Potentiators through my customized live keynotes, seminars and workshops.

ENVIRONICS/LIPKIN
RESEARCHED MOTIVATION & PERSUASION

33 BLOOR Street East, Suite 1020, Toronto, Ontario, Canada M4W 3H1

mikelipkin.com
mike.lipkin@environics.ca
1-416-969-2822

About the Author

MIKE LIPKIN is president of Environics/ Lipkin, a global research and motivation company based in Toronto. He is also an international strategic coach, guide and potentiator to leaders everywhere. His passion is creating breakthroughs with others by any means possible. He combines his personal experience of having talked to over a million people in 67 countries with his rigorous research on extraordinary performance. Mike was raised in Johannesburg, South Africa. He immigrated to Toronto, Canada, in 2001, where he now lives with his wife, Hilary. This is his eighth book.

Personal Reflections